Enter the Narrow Gate

Enter the Narrow Gate

Enter the
NARROW GATE

Saint Benedict's Steps to Christian Maturity

SUSAN MUTO

Our Sunday Visitor
Huntington, Indiana

Nihil Obstat
Msgr. Michael Heintz, Ph.D.
Censor Librorum

Imprimatur
✠ Kevin C. Rhoades
Bishop of Fort Wayne-South Bend
June 12, 2021

The *Nihil Obstat* and *Imprimatur* are official declarations that a book is free from doctrinal or moral error. It is not implied that those who have granted the *Nihil Obstat* and *Imprimatur* agree with the contents, opinions, or statements expressed.

Our Sunday Visitor Publishing Division
Our Sunday Visitor, Inc.
200 Noll Plaza
Huntington, IN 46750
www.osv.com
1-800-348-2440

ISBN: 978-1-68192-929-3 (Inventory No. T2671)
1. RELIGION—Christian Living—Spiritual Growth.
2. RELIGION—Christian Living—Inspirational.
3. RELIGION—Christianity—Catholic.
eISBN: 978-1-68192-930-9
LCCN: 2021936262

Cover and Interior design: Amanda Falk
Cover art: AdobeStock
Interior art: AdobeStock

PRINTED IN THE UNITED STATES OF AMERICA

Enter through the narrow gate;
for the gate is wide and the road
broad that leads to destruction, and those
who enter through it are many.
How narrow the gate and
constricted the road that leads
to life. And those who find it are few.

Matthew 7:13–14 (NABRE)

*The Strait Road — to live for others
in order to save one's soul.
The Broad — to live for others in order
to save one's self-esteem.*

*Dag Hammarskjöld
Markings*

Contents

Preface

This book is an invitation to every reader to enter through the narrow gate and not to be afraid of what awaits us. What drew me to write it was my desire to honor the memory of my spiritual friend and teacher of formative spirituality, the Rev. Adrian van Kaam, CSSp, Ph.D (1920–2007). Father Adrian left me, and so many students and colleagues, a legacy of how to enjoy life abundantly, and when the time came, of how to die in the grace and favor of the Lord.

In his diary, "The Blessing of a Coronary," written in May 1980, he wrote:

> God intends every event that happens to be for the best, especially in regard to those crucial transitions with which he graces us for the sake of drawing forth aspects of his divine form in our inmost being that would not be disclosed otherwise. A coronary is one such blessed event, one of great magnitude; it invites us to detach ourselves from a past form of life and to flow gently with grace into a new, more contemplative form of being.

About his own heart attack he said, as if he were forecasting his own death:

It is your tender knock on the door of my life: a sweet announcement of the life to come; of the joy and beauty of leaving this sinful earth; of the delight of death and dying; of the splendor of eternity; of the meeting with you face to Face. From now on this happiness may come to me at any moment, suddenly at night, during my sleep, walking in a street, teaching a class, or taking a bite of food. At any moment the great deliverance may be mine. In one blessed second it may all be over. Thank you, Lord. Thank you for this invitation to make myself ready for this lovely liberation.

If Father Adrian had had his own wishes, if he had not been so faithful to God's will for his life, he might have chosen a "gentle hermit's existence." This desire was fulfilled from 2005 to 2007 when he lived in the confinement of an aging, frail body likened to a desert experience readying him for God's lovely coming. Silently, gently, joyfully, he yielded during these months to his motto of *appreciative abandonment to the mystery*. I believe that this disposition, above all others, helped him to conserve his remaining energy so that together he could finish the body of work he had begun long ago in the Netherlands.

Even in his passing, he planted a message pertaining to the worthwhileness of his own and our life and labor. At the Little Sisters of the Poor, while living his "crucifying epiphany," he practiced the "ministry of the smile." Before God blew out the last flickering light of his burnt-up candle, Father relied on grace to sustain his efforts to serve God with every ounce of strength left to him.

In the course of editing his memoirs, I found the following diary entry in which he penned with stark honesty his struggle with the limits and the blessings of life. It reveals as well the depth and beauty of his humanity:

The coronary patient is not allowed to lose that last reservoir of energy in useless emotional, mental, or physical struggles, in hurry, heavy-mindedness, irritation,
or negative anticipation. It is surely not pleasing to you,
my Lord, if this inner dissonance … [dissipates] … the
task you ask your hermit to complete calmly and quiet-
ly before his joyous departure. This lack of detachment
would mar your servant's readiness for your coming;
it would stain the purity of his love and diminish the
compassion and surrender you want him to display in
all ways. Worse still, it would disperse and deplete his
life in useless passions. He would be unable to finish the
final assignments you impose on him at the end of his
short and perilous pilgrimage through this valley of sin,
suffering, illusion, and tears.

Father had only twenty-seven years left after his heart attack to
finish the task God had set before him. It meant so much to him
when he saw in print our four coauthored volumes on formation
theology. Shortly after the illnesses that required his admission
to round-the-clock skilled care, he told me: "I shall be glad to
leave and yet I must be faithful to my final tasks and to my loving
friends as long as God wants me to do so. With his grace I shall
bear the cross of this life as long as he desires. If I do or omit
anything to shorten it, it displeases my Lord. Alas, my time of
liberation is up to him alone."

    That time came at 9:00 p.m. on Saturday, November 17, 2007,
when Father Adrian surrendered himself fully to the height of
faith and the depth of human frailty God had allowed in his life.
The peace of Christ that passes understanding seemed to de-
scend upon his room where all of us gathered to bless him and
say farewell. Throughout the funeral proceedings over the next
several days, I reread these prophetic words I found in his diary:

Are you going to call me this night? I would love to see
you face to Face. But I feel sorry for those who may suffer
because of my leaving and sorry for a work still unfin-
ished. May your will be done. Good night, my Lord. Have
mercy on my soul. Above all, teach me to be less intense
in my thinking, planning, reading, speaking, imagining,
writing, and correcting, to be less impatient and more relaxed. What I need is the grace of holy equanimity.

That grace came to Father Adrian during the final week of his
earthly pilgrimage. His repeated advice to me, expressed with
and without words, was to ready myself "to sink away in the heart
of Jesus, into the immense, never threatening, always beckoning,
Divine Heart of the universe that treasures gently and joyously
all that is."

At the end of the eulogy I delivered at his funeral Mass, I felt
lifted in spirit to say:

Dear Father Adrian, we thank you for showing us how
to love God, how to live life to the full, and how to die
with serenity. Most of all, we thank you for being you.
May you enjoy the liberation of eternal blessedness
and may you be with us as we try with the help of grace
to live the Great Commandment, loving God and one
another, until that day when we meet him face to Face
and see in the mirror of the mystery who we were really meant to be.

Though your words can no longer be heard, your
spirit of faith, hope, and love embraces us and will always carry us along safe paths until our own time of
passing comes. Help us to keep courage as we await the
coming of the Lord whose boundless light surrounds
you now and forever. Amen.

From the start of our journey to its end, Father Adrian challenges us to find comfort in such paradoxes as power in powerlessness, joy in suffering, finding everything in nothing. I owe the inspiration for this book to him. Because he saw time as the antechamber to eternity, I will draw in *Enter the Narrow Gate* upon his life's work and legacy in the field of formative spirituality and especially upon the wisdom expressed in his prayer-poetry, which appears at the end of every step.

Allow me to acknowledge with immense gratitude the dedication of our administrative secretary, Gerrie Mullooly, who aided me in the production of this book. I thank also the many students who dared to ask, "What way ought we to follow?" The answers found here will reveal that the way is simple, not spectacular; it is gospel-rooted, not self-gratifying; it keeps us humble by reminding us that we are unworthy receivers of the awesome graces we have been given, knowing in Christ that "the last enemy to be destroyed is death" (1 Cor 15:26).

Twelve Steps to Heaven

A Road Map to the Narrow Way
Inspired by *The Rule of Saint Benedict*

*I am the gate. Whoever enters by me
will be saved, and will come in and
go out and find pasture.*

John 10:9

What is the meaning of the "narrow gate," and why does Jesus call himself the gate? How are we to find and pass through it? If life is a portal to paradise, then how to arrive there is everyone's concern. What we desire is to know, love, and serve God in this world that we may be happy with God in heaven.

Once we understand that we can only give to others what we have received from God, we stand at the entrance to the narrow way. What motivates us to give — not only of our abundance but also of the little we may have — is not routine politeness but a genuine concern to participate in one another's search for happiness. We relinquish our pride, read Scripture daily, and consult with masters of the spiritual life, who have trodden this path and want to share their experience with us.

One such master in the vast collection of Christian classics is St. Benedict of Nursia (480–547). In Chapter Seven of his *Rule,* he describes twelve steps to humility that can be read as a road map to the narrow way presented in this book. Each step provides a secure footing for us to find and stay on the path that Jesus tells us leads to life eternal. Each conveys virtues essential to becoming a true follower of the Master in contrast to the vices that block our way. Each shows us how to advance from the beginning stage of discipleship to the summit of conformity to Christ.

The story of Simon Peter exemplifies the struggle we face in following Christ. With no way of knowing what the future held, he dropped his fishing nets and followed Jesus. They became the best of friends, and yet one terrible night Peter denied the Master three times (see Lk 22:54–62). He veered from the narrow way to the broad road, but he had the humility to admit his mistake. He repented and sought forgiveness. He was to be, after all, the rock on which Christ would build his Church. Next consider Judas. He, too, walked with Jesus, who entrusted him with the apostles' purse. He accepted the Master as his teacher, but he withheld ultimate surrender to him as his Lord. He detoured from the path of redemption, never to return. His own plan failed, and death was his only alternative.

The narrow way refers, as in the case of Peter, to our intention to follow Jesus, not whimsically but as a way of life, even though we deviate from it once in a while. That is when and why we rely on the mercy of Jesus to correct the wrong course we have temporarily taken. The narrow gate signifies our standing before the entrance to this saving path and having to decide between it and the broad road that leads, as in the case of Judas, to a life that rejects Jesus as Lord. In other words, we enter through the narrow gate in the conviction that the narrow way will become our lifelong goal.

In this book, I present the "how to" of avoiding "destruction" of life's meaning so that at life's end God may find us worthy to enjoy the grace of a happy death radiant with the hope of heaven.

Part One recognizes that we are treasures in clay jars (see 2 Cor 4:7), always in need of ongoing transformation. To evade the comforts of the broad path and stay on the narrow way entails ongoing conversion illumined by the first four steps of *The Rule of Saint Benedict.* Part Two shows us the struggle we face in choosing the rigors of the hard road and experiencing both the desolations and the consolations of discipleship. Here we follow steps five through eight. Then in Part Three (steps nine to twelve), having entered the gate, we advance in prayerful surrender toward union with the Trinity in the light of our dying and rising with the Lord.

Only by keeping the exercise of humility in the forefront of our consciousness can we move from self-exaltation to a state of likeness to Christ in our internal and external life. Chapter Seven of Saint Benedict's *Rule* provides twelve steps that we should follow in our advance from the beginning stages of discipleship to the summit of conformity to Christ as active contemplatives and contemplatives-in-action. In my book *A Feast for Hungry Souls,* I trace these steps as follows:

1. *Holy fear.* The first step or mark of Christian maturity is keeping the fear of God always before our eyes, which helps us to avoid sin and monitor our decisions and deeds from God's perspective. Holy fear inspires us to reevaluate our actions in regard to both personal prayer and community participation. According to Benedict, we must always be fearful of allowing selfish motives to weaken the in-

fluence of God's Word in our everyday life. We must remember God's commandments and consider the fact that God always beholds us from heaven. Our actions are everywhere visible to our heavenly Father. To live in awe, remembering that without God we can do nothing, prevents us from becoming excessively preoccupied with worldly power, pleasure, and possession.

2. *Surrender of the will.* The second step emphasizes that we should not love our own will or take pleasure in the satisfaction of selfish desires; rather we must imitate Christ's actions and say with the Lord: "I have come ... not to do my own will, but the will of him who sent me" (Jn 6:38). Being detached from our own willful desires means being attached to God's guiding grace. Not loving our own will makes us less vulnerable to being entrapped by self-centered motivations. We avoid any behavior that is not inspired by humble cooperation with the infinite grace that enlightens our finite nature.

3. *Obedience.* The third step or degree of humility requires submission to our superiors (a bishop, a pastor, or a spiritual director, to give a few examples) in imitation of the obedience of Jesus to his Father's will. As we read in Philippians 2:8, he "became obedient to the point of death — even death on a cross." Obedience counters the notion of personal autonomy and the egocentric assumption that "I am the master of my fate, / I am the captain of my soul." All such illusions erode the spiritual maturity essential for discipleship. This step counters the notion of personal autonomy and the egocentric assumption that we are in charge. It counsels us to accept the

limitations and directives placed upon us by legitimate authority.

4. *Endurance in suffering.* Exercised in favorable as well as unfavorable circumstances, obedience forecasts the fourth step: being willing to embrace suffering with patience and endure it for Christ's sake without weakening or seeking to escape. This step requires that we deny ourselves for the sake of carrying life's crosses in the certitude that under difficult, unfavorable, or even unjust conditions they will draw us to deeper intimacy with the Lord. Rather than willfully exercising impatient control and resisting the challenges posed by our daily crosses, we embrace them with a sense of trust and docility.

5. *Unguarded confession.* The fifth step reminds us of the importance of not concealing from our confessors any of our sinful thoughts and wrongdoings. A humble confession, full of integrity, allows us, as Psalm 37 says, to make known our ways to the Lord and hope in him: "Commit your way to the LORD; / trust in him, and he will act. / He will make your vindication shine like the light, / and the justice of your cause like the noonday" (Ps 37:5–6). Then, too, Psalm 32 reminds us that we will experience God's forgiveness to the degree that we acknowledge our faults and offenses: "While I kept silence, my body wasted away through my groaning all day long. For day and night your hand was heavy upon me; my strength was dried up as by the heat of summer. Then I acknowledged my sin to you, / and I did not hide my iniquity; / I said, 'I will confess my transgressions to the LORD,' / and you forgave the guilt of my sin" (Ps 32:3–5). By acknowledging and

confessing our faults and failings, we cultivate compunction of heart and refinement of conscience.

6. *Contentment in humiliation.* The outcome of these first five steps happens on the sixth rung of the ladder of humility, which enables mature Christians to be content with the lowest and most menial tasks. The desire to be insignificant and no better than a beast of burden before the Lord cancels all prideful attempts to be the boss! Tasks we once found to be annoying or tedious have a profound meaning when we consider ourselves no more than worthless servants (see Lk 17:10). By neither grumbling when we do not get our way nor blaming others for our problems, we learn to accept unfair treatment and misunderstanding with a gracious heart while maintaining respect for others.

7. *Self-abasement and utter dependence upon God's providence.* The seventh step interiorizes this feeling of unworthiness and deepens the awareness of our depending on God for everything. It gives us the courage to declare in speech and to witness in action the simple truth that we are lower and of less importance than others, echoing the words of the psalmist, "It is good for me that I was humbled, / so that I might learn your statues" (Ps 119:71). Instead of discounting the extent of our arrogance or secretly seeing ourselves as better than others, we see every opportunity for humbling, even for humiliation, as a blessing that enables us to let go of all self-centeredness and to put on the mind of Christ (see 1 Cor 2:16).

8. *Avoiding singularity and living the common ways revealed by Christ.* The eighth step of Saint Benedict's

ladder of humility reveals a penchant in our heart to efface ourselves by pointing instead to Christ. We foster a wise blending of solitude and togetherness, of silence and speaking, of worship and work. We adhere to the common ways of liturgy, word, and sacrament and do not expect to receive privileges and special treatments. In short, on this step we try not to draw attention to ourselves since we are content with the ordinary blessings of everyday life.

9. *Custody of speech and keeping silence.* The ninth degree of humility concerns the importance of restraining our tongue and keeping silence until we need to answer questions or offer counsel to others. Saint Benedict agreed with the proverbial truth that "when words are many, transgression is not lacking" (Prv 10:19). This step cautions us not to engage in empty, idle chatter, nor to give in to the inclination to fill up silence with noise. The *Rule* wants us to use words and the gift of speech for the purpose of edifying others. As the apostle James warns, the tongue can be "a restless evil, full of deadly poison" (Jas 3:8).

10. *Not engaging in derisive laughter or cynical humor.* Common as it may be to mock those following the narrow way, such derision is as foolish as it is unbecoming. It can condone gossip and discourage sober, realistic commitment to Christ. Gentle humor, rooted in humility, fosters mutual encouragement and replaces murmuring and complaining with patience and modesty.

11. *Dignified comportment.* The more we learn to speak gently, without sarcasm or cynicism, the more we comport ourselves as Christ's followers in this world.

We preach the Gospel by our presence and, in the spirit of St. Francis of Assisi, we may or may not need to use words. Having banned all depreciative patterns of speech, we carry ourselves with dignity, respecting others and communicating words of wisdom with the dignified comportment they foster.

12. *Walk with reverence of heart in the truth of who we are.* On the twelfth rung, in both thought and action, we are humble in the depths of our heart, open to the truth in our mind, and ready to do what God wills in daily life. To follow this classical master's steps of humility leads to a change of life that comprises a blueprint for Christian maturity in our own and every age. Because we try our best to manifest humility in our behavior, we help to dispel in those around us the illusion of self-sufficiency. Sinners though we may be, we know that we are beloved by God. To paraphrase Saint Benedict's prayer in Chapter Seventy-Two, "May we value nothing whatever above Christ himself and may he bring us all together to eternal life."

Having climbed the ladder of humility under the tutelage of Saint Benedict, we may wonder why these twelve steps are not merely for monastics but for all of us in today's world. We can offer the answer by asking: Who of us would not benefit from restoring the disposition of awe; from renouncing our own self-centered willfulness; from refusing to listen to the wise and experienced guides among us; from being more patient in times of suffering; from feeling deep sorrow for our sins; from ceasing to play the blame game; from calling more attention to the good deeds of others than to our own; from restraining our tongue; from avoiding sarcastic derision and gossipy put-downs; from carrying ourselves with dignity; and from cultivating humility of heart?

When we focus our eyes on these goals, we are able to avoid sinful detours and monitor our decisions and deeds from God's perspective. We choose not to engage in behavior inspired by selfishness but by humble cooperation with divine grace. Obedience to God's will must be exercised in favorable as well as unfavorable circumstances, when the sun shines and when storms cut open ruts in the road. We know in faith that obeying God in this way draws us to deeper intimacy with the Trinity. Thinking about how and why we may be inclined to disobey the Lord lessens the fear that we may lose our way. Instead we welcome every opportunity to let go of lingering traces of egocentric control. With the psalmist we say, "I am your servant; give me understanding, / so that I may know your decrees" (Ps 119:125).

With each step along the way, our joy increases. We mirror the Master and become his instruments of justice, peace, and mercy in this world. We control our tongue and temper, the tendency to be too talkative or to engage in idle gossip or incessant grumbling. To follow the lead of grace is to behold in awe the full meaning of the Divine Adventure that inspired us to enter through the narrow gate. It is so that we might "Keep [our] steps steady according to your promise, / and never let iniquity have dominion over [us]" (Ps 119:133), and so we pray:

Thank you, Father, for sending your Word into this world:

for reminding us every day that we must live from the center of our humility;

for teaching us that in every limit there resides a blessing you invite us to behold;

for giving us the greatest gift anyone on earth could receive: your body and your blood, the food of life, the chalice of salvation;

for letting what we do be an expression of who we are;

for the cosmic wonder of this world, for your knowing the number of the stars and calling them all by name;

for living with us as one of us in all things but sin;

for helping us learn from our mistakes, confess our sins, and ask for forgiveness;

for urging us to seek ways to improve our life and never become complacent;

for giving us solace in music, friends, and good meals, in the beauty of the natural world and in the joy of quiet contemplation of your first revelation in creation;

for messages of love given and received as vivid reminders that you are love and that despite the pain of loneliness, we are never alone;

for telling us not to be afraid, for you are with us always, even to the end of the world;

for the blessed assurance that in every end is a new beginning and that in every obstacle there is a formation opportunity.

Part One

Evade the Comforts of the Wide Road

But we have this treasure in clay jars, so that it may be made clear that this extraordinary power belongs to God and does not come from us. We are afflicted in every way, but not crushed; perplexed, but not driven to despair; persecuted, but not forsaken; struck down, but not destroyed; always carrying in the body the death of Jesus, so that the life of Jesus may also be made visible in our bodies. For while we live, we are always being given up to death for Jesus' sake, so that the life of Jesus may be made visible in our mortal flesh. So death is at work in us, but life in you.

2 Corinthians 4:7–12

STEP ONE
Cultivate Holy Fear

Awakening to the Reality
of Who We Are

*Happy are those whose way is blameless,
who walk in the law of the LORD.*

Psalm 119:1

Proverbs 1:7 proclaims that fear of the Lord is the beginning
of wisdom, and the Book of Revelation adds this imperative:
"Fear God and give him glory" (14:7). To eschew the comforts
of the broad path that leads to destruction, we must awaken to
the reality of who we are. That is why Benedict's first step on the
ladder of humility encourages us to remember God's commandments and live in awe of God's beholding us from on high. On
the road to destruction, we act as if we are gods; on the road that
leads to life, we know we are mere creatures of God, fallen, to

be sure, but worthy of forgiveness by virtue of the fact that our "delight is in the law of the LORD" (Ps 1:2).

Immediately, a paradox presents itself. The entrance to the way may be narrow, but it is wide enough to encompass the whole of who we are: God made us children in his image and likeness (see Gn 1:27) and from the beginning of time loved us enough to liberate us from the perilous traps of sin and self-deception. In holy fear or awe, we hear God say to us in the words of the prophet Hosea, "I will heal their disloyalty; / I will love them freely" (Hos 14:4). As much as broken bones need mending and crushed spirits need uplifting, so creatures as fallible and finite as we are need healing, both physically and spiritually.

During his public ministry, Jesus cleansed lepers, enabled the blind to see and the deaf to hear, cast out demons, and brought people back from the dead. Even to touch the hem of his garment was to be made whole (see Mt 9:20). Though the cures we seek may or may not be forthcoming, our faith in the Divine Healer never wavers. It prevents us from succumbing to despair. Sick in body and soul as we may be, what matters is to keep the faith that allowed us to enter through the narrow gate in the first place.

Having passed through this entry point, we are in awe of the treasure in clay jars that we are. Our inner life is the place of the heart where we discover, despite our sinfulness, how inspiring our journey has been. Encounters along the way — in family life, Church, and society — have both formed and deformed us, drawn us closer to Christ and at times cast us farther away, but all have shown us another facet of the diamond of divinity we truly are. Holy fear allowed us to discern what situations were harmful and which were helpful for living in Christ. The latter opened us to receive inspirations from the Holy Spirit that led to deeper discipleship; the former put us at risk of losing our way by resisting or refusing God's grace.

To be a spiritual person is to ponder, both intentionally and at unexpected times, our eternal destiny. These reflections influence the choices we make. They reveal that the gate to salvation is open to all, but its entrance is narrow. Pebbles of humility, self-sacrifice, and poverty line the way, and walking on them often hurts our feet. The path to perdition, on the other hand, is smoothly paved. No wonder we desire to take it, but what promises to be life-giving ends up being life-denying.

Consider this passage from the Gospel of Matthew (which precedes Jesus' invitation to enter through the narrow gate in Matthew 7:13). After telling us to look at the birds of the air whom the Father feeds, and at the lilies of the field that neither toil nor spin, Christ concludes that we ought not to worry about what to eat or drink or wear, adding this imperative: "Strive first for the kingdom of God and his righteousness, and all these things will be given to you" (Mt 6:33).

Two choices stand before us: to follow Jesus and receive all that we need to stay on the heavenly way, or to abandon him and end up with nothing. Either we strive first for the kingdom or we don't. Either we enter through the narrow gate and live in, with, and through Christ, or we roam without rhyme or reason on the road to destruction. Either we find a portal to heaven in the heart of God, or we meander onto the path of perdition. There is no compromise possible. As the psalmist says: "For a day in your courts is better than a thousand elsewhere. / I would rather be a doorkeeper in the house of my God / than live in the tents of wickedness" (Ps 84:10).

Awakening to the "Givens" We Receive

There are some facets of our life over which we have no control — they are simply "givens." One "given" is the time and place in which we are born: Antarctica or Africa; Oregon or Oklahoma;

the Northeast or the deep South; a family of poverty or wealth; illiterate or educated; religious or atheist.

This underlying setting — the climate, the culture, the family, the tradition — where we come into existence is a form of "narrowness" that will be with us for the rest of our lives. Jesus, being fully human, is no different in this regard. He was born of Mary in Bethlehem. He was a Nazarene. His foster father was a carpenter. He grew up near the Sea of Galilee. He was a Jew, who had studied the Torah and was able to discuss its teaching with the elders in the Temple.

Another "given" occurs in the womb of our mother. It is our physical self with its unique biogenetic profile: white, black, brown; tall, thin, short, chubby; healthy or sickly; good or poor eyesight; a specific bodily constitution; and a temperament — sweet, sour, shy, outgoing. Our five senses, seeing, hearing, touching, tasting, and smelling, be they intact or impaired by blindness or deafness, enable us to react and respond to our environment while we strive to mature in wisdom, age, and grace as did the Lord.

We humans are doers. The functional "givens" of our life account for our gifts, talents, and skills. "He was already playing the piano at three." "She could collect a batch of dry leaves and turn them into a work of art." "He only had to see a word once and he would never forget how to spell it." "She always knew how to select matching accessories for any outfit she wore."

Such "givens" have an indelible effect on our mind and will. They influence the choice we make to walk through the narrow gate and persevere under the guidance of the Master. They inspire us to do unto others what we hope they will do for us.

Permeating all of these "givens" is our openness in holy fear to the Sacred in whom "we live and move and have our being" (Acts 17:28). Here we ponder what ultimately matters to us and how best to accomplish our goals in response to the grace of

God. Here the Holy Spirit opens our human spirit to the Scriptures and teaches us how to listen to Jesus and follow his call.

To cultivate holy fear is to let go of the remnants of selfish sensuality so that we can evade the comforts of the wide path and go through the narrow gate that leads to a good life and a happy death.

Awakening to the Dynamics of Walking the Way with Christ

The inspirations of the Holy Spirit draw us to ponder who we are, from whence we have come, and where God wants us to go. We ask as well whether or not our actions are effective, our services charitable, our yearnings to be with God never satisfied with less.

To walk the way with Christ is to pursue a life that is both pleasing to God and uplifting for God's people. It is to heed the invitation of the psalmist, "Enter his gates with thanksgiving, / and his courts with praise. / Give thanks to him, bless his name" (Ps 100:4).

Cultivating holy fear prompts us to be creative and committed so that the good works we do for the Lord bear lasting fruit (see Jn 15:16). Our purpose through every activity is to serve the greater honor and glory of God. That is why we shun blind ambitions associated with power-mongering or excessive possessiveness.

To know ourselves as God knows us is to take into account our physical limits and gifts while controlling compulsions that may lead to addictive patterns of behavior. We aim to align our life with our heart's desire for God and with the teachings found in Holy Scripture and the writings of the spiritual masters. As long as attaining heaven is our life's aim, we are less prone to fall for the fads that fill the airways, appear on billboards, and prove to be here today and gone tomorrow. What concerns us is to discern what is and what is not of value for our overall well-being.

To acquire possessions whether we need them or not, to feel pleasure that gratifies mere lustful desires, or to promote ambitions to gain power pale in comparison to our longing to live in conformity to the gospel truths for which our Lord himself lived and died. He gives us the courage to enter the narrow gate and to choose those virtues that alone can give us a taste on earth of the happiness that will be ours in heaven.

Awakening to the Integration of Who We Are with What We Do

Committing ourselves to follow Christ through the narrow gate is rewarding but risky. We are not always able to predict where our call will lead us. Mysterious as it is to follow the narrow way, every step we take challenges us to respond with faith, hope, and love to the unexpected. Choosing one way of listening to the Lord may limit us from selecting another, but once we decide to walk through this gate, the love of Christ draws us onward to eternity.

To fulfill the spiritual purpose of our existence, no matter what happens to us, be it good or bad, depends on God's guidance. Grace elevates our dispersed lives to new heights of union and communion with God and to a sense of the true significance of every person, event, and thing we encounter.

Just as the petal of a rose blends into the fullness of its perfection, so each thread of life weaves itself into every other, forming a harmonious whole. Cultivating holy fear has awakened us to the reality of who we are and has taught us to abide with the mystery at the center of our being. We see in God's light all that we are and hope to be, and so we pray:

Jesus,
Let me remain in you
as you remain in me.
Be a source of fruitfulness
in my niche in history.
To carry fruit abundantly
delights the Father's eye.
He looks at us so tenderly,
he smiles on me,
alive in you,
a servant of humanity.
Fill me with your words,
those shining bridges
that like rainbows
harmonize my doings
with the heaven of your presence.
Let them penetrate my busy mind,
my dried-up soul,
like fragrant oil.
If you grant me a fleeting sense
of your abiding,
let me not clutch it greedily
but flow gently with the mystery
of your appearance and departure
in my daily life.

Pause and Ponder

- In what way does holy fear help me to awaken to the self-knowledge that leads to knowledge of God?
- Can I honestly say that I am living in awe and in fidelity to Christ's call? If not, do I have the courage to examine my conscience and change course?

STEP TWO
Imitate Christ and Seek His Will

Obeying the Word of the Lord

Happy are those who keep his decrees,
who seek him with their whole heart,
who also do no wrong,
but walk in his ways.

Psalm 119:2–3

Life is for the most part a series of choices — from where we live, work, and raise a family to how we age (gracefully or enraged by our limits) and how we welcome or curse the reality of death.

Though the way Christ exemplifies is often difficult to choose, it proves to be the best one to follow. As Saint Benedict reminds us in the second step of humility, we need to renounce the temptation to delight in fulfilling our own desires, saying with the Lord, "I have come ... not to do my own will, but the will of him who sent me" (Jn 6:38). He leaves us free to run away from his teaching and resist the grace that enables us to listen to it, but we may come to regret the consequences of these choices.

The narrow way paradoxically widens our perspective on the goodness of life as a whole, whereas the road to perdition shrinks our options and never profits us in the long run. That is why the Bible confronts us with such classical questions of choice as: "For what will it profit them if they gain the whole world but forfeit their life? Or what will they give in return for their life?" (Mt 16:26).

In his Christian classic, *The Cost of Discipleship*, Dietrich Bonhoeffer addresses the "great divide" we who choose to imitate Christ must face. Will we follow the narrow way of testifying to the truth or the wide path of compromise to please the world? Will we put our hopes in personal achievements, or will we pay the price to remain faithful to Jesus?

Bonhoeffer walked on the razor's edge between the worldliness of the world and the kingdom of heaven, between the broad road and the constricted way that leads to life. This way is seldom predictable. How could Dietrich have foreseen that he would be martyred by the Nazi gestapo? He gives witness to what it means to live in faithfulness wherever God places us. We seek his will and obey his word, convinced of the truth of these prophetic words: "For there is still a vision for the appointed time; / it speaks of the end, and does not lie. / If it seems to tarry, wait for it; / it will surely come, it will not delay" (Hab 2:3).

The poet Robert Frost beheld a similar divide in his poem "The Road Not Taken." There he depicts two pathways diverging in a "yellow wood." Interested as he was to walk on both of them, he had to make a choice. Though one way looked worn but fair, he chose "the one less traveled by, / And that has made all the difference." The analogy to the narrow way is striking; it is less familiar and more challenging to traverse. Choosing it leads us to our longed-for destination. Attractive as the road that leads to destruction may be, strong as its pull, we must turn away from it, lest it entangle us in nets of iniquity from which God's grace alone can free us.

Imitating Our Lord

To imitate Christ and to evade the channels of perdition that prevent us from loving others as he has loved us (see 1 Jn 3:23) is a lifelong endeavor. We express this love by respecting life, by abandoning useless worry, and by walking in the truth that "the LORD is [our] light and [our] salvation" (Ps 27:1). We are the servants our Master befriends and upon whom he bestows the blessing of unconditional love. He commands us to be forgiving, compassionate, and caring. He wants us to live in the world without being of the world. We must become childlike by growing in trust and simplicity and by relating to God as "Abba." How grateful we are to be "children ... of God" and "joint heirs with Christ — ... [who] suffer with him so that we may also be glorified with him" (Rom 8:17). As Bonhoeffer notes, the very narrowness of the road increases our certainty that this is where we belong and that only through bondage to Christ can we be set free.

The highest efficacy of the narrow way is that on it we will pass "from death to life" (1 Jn 3:14). Only then, albeit after a lifetime of searching, with many endings and new beginnings, will we "find rest for [our] souls" (Mt 11:29). Unrestful would be any attempt to act in ways at odds with our true self. To know who Jesus is, is to know who we are.

There are many "I am" descriptions of Christ in Holy Scripture: Prince of Peace, Good Shepherd, Bread of Life. Jesus gathers all these descriptions into one when he says to the apostles, "I am the way, and the truth, and the life. No one comes to the

Father except through me" (Jn 14:6).

The more we come to know who we are with our faults and failings, our gifts and blessings, the more we realize how much we need our merciful Lord to understand and forgive us. Who of us would not agree with Simon Peter, who fell at the feet of Jesus after the miraculous catch of fish that filled his boat to the sinking point, saying: "Go away from me, Lord, for I am a sinful man!" (Lk 5:8).

Compassion binds us to Jesus and to the faith community he founded. To persevere on the narrow way, we rely on one another and most of all on the forgiveness of our merciful Lord, beseeching the Spirit to help us in our weakness (see Rom 8:26).

God's call is not a commodity we have; it is who we are. Since we cannot enflesh our call at once, its incarnation has to be ongoing. We never accomplish it; we are forever achieving it. That is why we identify with John the Baptist every time we say: "I am not worthy to untie the thong of the sandals on his feet" (Acts 13:25).

The more we come to know who we are with our faults and failings, our gifts and blessings, the more we realize how difficult it is and will be for us to live a godly life in surrender to the Father. We will be part of a "little flock" in contrast to the colossal number who prefer to pursue self-indulgence and ignore the perdition that is the result of their making idols of power, pleasure, and possession.

The call to imitate Christ is not a badge of honor we acquire; it is a sure sign of our destiny in response to the Infinite Love that beckoned us forth out of nothingness and redeemed the identity we lost due to sin.

Fidelity to our call is not a static formula but a dynamic response to the situations where God places us. In the swirling sea of everydayness, there are many broken shells, bits of seaweed and scattered debris. Although we may desire to seek a cleaner beach, this is where God wants us to walk.

As we follow Saint Benedict's guidance in seeking to imitate Christ, we benefit from the sage advice of another spiritual master. In her book *The Way of Perfection*, Doctor of the Church St. Teresa of Ávila (1515–1582) outlines three dynamics of discipleship that lead us to hear and heed the word of the Lord.

Love for one another, not tainted by selfishness but so unselfish that no sacrifice is too much to ask of us, is the first order to follow if we want to live in imitation of the selfless love of our Savior. That is why Saint Teresa advises us to keep his sacred humanity before our eyes, so that we can see what obedience to his commandment to "love one another" (Jn 13:34) really means.

Detachment from created things comes next. It is an inclusive virtue, meaning that it lets us exclude as ultimate what is not of God. It guards us against being possessed by our possessions. They come and go, rise and fall, stay for a while and pass away. If we become overly absorbed in them, we lose our freedom to imitate Christ's obedience to the Father's will. If we want union with our Lord, and through him to gain everything worthwhile, we must seek detachment from any lesser good as absolute. Without this virtue of detachment, we are likely to become victims of worldly ambitions and erratic impulses that cause us to forget, in the words of Saint Teresa, that "God alone suffices."

Humility is the foundation of love for others and detachment from things. It guards us from demonic temptations to follow the dictates of pride and the vain reasonings that lead to an endless search for self-satisfaction. Great progress on the way of perfection occurs when we take on lowly tasks; avoid the privileges of rank and power; disengage ourselves from excesses of praise or blame; and bear with dishonor, ridicule, and misunderstanding. Only then can we model our lives on the humility displayed by Jesus, not wavering from the way for reasons of worldly honor, but weighing whatever we say and do in the light of what God asks of us.

Seeking God's Will on the Narrow Way

There are times when it seems as if we cannot walk one more step. We feel like bruised, broken reeds that the slightest breeze can blow over. And yet we rise and go on because, in ways seen and unseen, we know that the Lord carries us as he carried his cross to Calvary. Our weakness comes as no surprise to him. Our shame attracts his forgiveness, our misery his mercy. Our life, with its sufferings and joys, becomes an offering of sacrificial love to the Father through Jesus under the advocacy of the Holy Spirit.

Even when the way passes through the darkest valley, we fear no evil because *the* Way is with us. With his rod and his staff he comforts us (see Ps 23:4). We act not on the basis of our own merits but on the strength of our obedience to God's will.

One fruit of obeying the Lord is our ability to empathize with what others are going through. We accept them as they are and support their choice to evade the comforts of the broad path. Such empathy extends as well to those who have not chosen the narrow path. We learn not to judge them but to pray for them. We ask the Lord to be merciful to them and to lead them in accordance with his will to the joy of salvation. We engage in sincere, open-hearted exchanges about our motives for ministry and our respect for the dignity of life. We face with courage the misgivings that used to sap our energy and drain away our hope. We celebrate together the joy that is ours in Jesus, a joy that lasts amid suffering and that outlasts every passing gratification. We remind one another that the work we do must never lose its connection to the Lord for whom we labor.

If such are the signs of seeking God's will, then what are those that show our veering toward the path that leads to destruction? They include a duplicitous disconnection between what we say and how we act. Our demeanor becomes more rigid and less graceful. Our action is strained, our emotion frustrated, our productivity curtailed. A domineering tone creeps into our voice. Those we intended to serve sense on some level that we do not really care about them. They are only pawns in our business enterprises. We pretend to support them to secure their compliance with little or no show of genuine appreciation for them.

Receptivity to the deeper meaning of the tasks we perform may not change them, but it does alter our attitude toward service as an expression of conformity to Christ. What we do becomes a response to Jesus' invitation: "Come away to a deserted place all by yourselves and rest a while" (Mk 6:31).

Obeying the Word of the Lord

The Lord issues this simple invitation, "Come," many times in the Gospels: Come and see. Come you who labor and are heavy-burdened. Come, follow me. The key to understanding and accepting his call to rest resides in the words "away by yourselves" and "rest awhile." Jesus invites us to be alone with him so that we can distinguish his voice amid a cacophony of sounds and replenish our capacity to defend the sacred significance of the least among us. Deserted as the narrow way may be, that is where we meet Jesus.

Consider how important it is for us to obey the word of the Lord as proclaimed in the Book of Deuteronomy. God sets before the chosen people the way they must go if they want to prosper. God invites them to show the world what it means to love their Creator with their whole heart and soul. Two roads loom before them. One is wide and leads to destruction. The other is narrow and leads to life.

Prior to setting before them the right standard to follow,

God assures them that the choice they have to make is not re-
mote; it is right in front of them. They do not need to go up to
heaven to find it. Neither is it beyond the sea and out of their
reach. The way is near to them, as near as God's word, which is
in their mouth and written on their heart. Which way will they
choose?

> See, I have set before you today life and prosperity,
> death and adversity. If you obey the commandments of
> the LORD your God that I am commanding you today,
> by loving the LORD your God, walking in his ways, and
> observing his commandments, decrees, and ordinances,
> then you shall live. ... But if your heart turns away and
> you do not hear, but are led astray ... you shall not live.
> ... I have set before you life and death, blessings and
> curses. Choose life so that you and your descendants
> may live. (Deuteronomy 30:15–19)

This choice is not a once and for all decision, but one we must
make every day. Proverbs 18:21 reminds us that "death and life
are in the power of the tongue." Gossips who couldn't care less
about destroying another's reputation have chosen death whether they know it or not. A person who tries to avoid gossip and
ends every conversation on a complimentary note has chosen
life. Think of how many times this scene repeats itself around
kitchen tables and in office corridors.

The wide road to destruction lurks around every corner.
We must be vigilant to spot it and run the other way. Saint Paul
reminds us in 2 Corinthians 3:6 that "the letter kills, but the
Spirit gives life." The Pharisees and Sadducees knew the letter
of the law inside out, but because the Author of Life, Jesus,
did not conform to it as they thought he should (for instance,
he allowed his disciples to pluck and eat grain on the Sabbath

[see Mt 12:1-2]), they plotted to kill him. Had they not studied the writings of the Prophet Isaiah? Did they not find in them these comforting, life-changing words? "Comfort, O comfort my people, says your God. / Speak tenderly to Jerusalem, and cry to her / that she has served her term, / that her penalty is paid, / that she has received from the LORD's hand / double for all her sins" (Is 40:1–2).

Unless we obey the Lord's word, we may detour into the dense underbrush of perdition. But fear not! In these wilderness experiences, the Holy Spirit readies another clearing and returns us to the narrow way. With Christ at our side, we have the courage to carry on. Even when overwhelming odds confront us, we thank God for being at our side and for helping us to stay the course he outlines for us: "Proclaim the word; be persistent whether it is convenient or inconvenient; convince, reprimand, encourage through all patience and teaching" (2 Tm 4:2, NABRE).

In this text there are five "little commandments" that confirm what happens to us when we follow the way of the Lord as Timothy did when he abided by Paul's instructions:

1. *Proclaim the Word.* That means ponder the Scriptures daily. Let these truths become so much a part of our lives that we choose not to argue about them but to proclaim them to anyone with ears to hear. As we read in Matthew 10:27, "What I say to you in the dark, tell in the light; and what you hear whispered, proclaim from the housetops."

2. *Be persistent.* In a word, this imperative means to persevere, to go forward. Whether what needs to be done is convenient or inconvenient, we do it anyway because that is what the Lord asks of us. As we read in Hebrews 12:1–2, "let us run with perseverance

the race that is set before us, looking to Jesus the pioneer and perfecter of our faith."

3. *Convince.* We can only do this if we live what we profess. We convince not merely with the words on our lips but with the virtues of faith, hope, and love in our hearts. Our actions need to be consistent, not guided by whimsical moods or "political correctness" but by rock-solid convictions of the truths Jesus teaches.

4. *Reprimand.* There is a tendency in all of us to go along with what pleases people, but at times we have no choice but to engage in fraternal admonition. Our yes has to mean *yes,* and our no has to mean *no.* There is and will always be a difference between right and wrong, so we cannot avoid an occasional and appropriate reprimand. Ours is not a posture of self-righteousness but a genuine concern for helping people find the right path to salvation. Admonition is also reciprocal. We need to be open to receive reprimands from others. Moments like these can be painful, but gracious acceptance of well-meant criticism is necessary for our spiritual growth.

5. *Encourage through all patience and teaching.* What complements a needed reprimand must be an equally necessary encouragement. People do not change overnight. We need to be patient with those whom we try to teach. This was Jesus' way with his disciples, and so must it be ours. Discouragement erodes proclaiming, being persistent, convincing, and reprimanding. Encouraging words bolster these actions and offer people the courage they need to follow Jesus. As Paul emphasizes in Philippians 2:1–

2, "If then there is any encouragement in Christ, any consolation from love, any sharing in the Spirit, any compassion and sympathy, make my joy complete: be of the same mind, having the same love, being in full accord and of one mind."

And so we pray:

Holy Mystery of Divinity,
  let me learn from you
  gentleness of heart.
Free me from arrogance,
  from goals too sublime for me.
Still and quiet my soul
  as a mother quiets the little ones on her lap.
Free me from needs for achievement.
Make my life less forceful, more gentle.
Let the splendor of your presence
  light up my everydayness.
Make me harmonize my finite spirit with the Infinite
    Spirit
  who fills universe and history.

Love Divine,
  invade my soul,
  melt every trace of vehemence,
  so that I may be a smooth channel for the outflow
  of your holy Word in this world.

Pause and Ponder

- Do I appreciate the fact that to enter the narrow gate in imitation of Christ is a journey of discovery based on my listening to God's plan for my own and others' well-being?
- Do I know in the depths of my heart that I must rely on grace to lead me from the path of perdition to the cleansing, redemptive blessings found on the narrow way?

STEP THREE
Submit to Legitimate Authority

Abiding by Directives of Discipleship

O that my ways may be steadfast
in keeping your statutes!

Psalm 119:5

When we journey to a place where we have never been before, we seek the best directions we can find. We study maps, talk to people who have traveled there, program our GPS, and choose where we can stop for food and rest for the night. We trust that the directions we have received are correct and that we will reach our destination. We have no reason to doubt such legitimate sources of guidance and every reason to abide by what we have learned.

Once we have chosen to enter through the narrow gate, we

47

recognize with each step we traverse how much guidance we need. It is fitting that Saint Benedict's third step on the ladder of humility is obedience. He asks us to be mindful of the example set by Jesus, who "became obedient to the point of death" (Phil 2:8). We have every reason to thank God for the inspiration and information we receive daily from our faith and formation traditions. We ask our Divine Guide for the grace to go forward and never reverse course. We notice how the way simplifies our life and increases our care for others. Walking stills the unabated noise that distracts us from meditation and ministry. Though bombarded by the "babel" of social media and the agitation it foments, we remember that we are temples of the living God (see 2 Cor 6:16–18); we are God's ambassadors, "since God is making his appeal through us ... so that in him we might become the righteousness of God" (2 Cor 5:20–21).

Abiding by Our Calling in Christ

God is like a good gardener, who selects the seeds (our life's call) that will blossom in the pristine sunlight of spring (our vocation and its many avocations) in personal and social life. Anything that happens to us along the way is an opportunity, which God gives or allows, to make us more aware of what he has in mind for us. Each happening contains some expression of the providential meaning God intends for our lives as a whole. This divine direction unfolds between our birth and our transition to eternity after the pilgrimage God destines for us on earth.

The narrow way in which Christ calls us to walk matches perfectly the little way of spiritual childhood described by St. Thérèse of Lisieux in her autobiography, *The Story of a Soul.* Inspiring her were the biblical passages she loved, notably the Gospel of John and the epistles of Paul. She lived the three virtues detailed by St. Teresa of Ávila in *The Way of Perfection*: love for one another, detachment, and humility, all of which confirmed her littleness and God's greatness.

In John's Gospel, Jesus asks us to make a choice: "Abide in me as I abide in you. Just as the branch cannot bear fruit by itself unless it abides in the vine, neither can you unless you abide in me" (Jn 15:4). This condition facilitates our calling in Christ, as Saint Thérèse realized. To remain in the Lord means both to worship him in the silence of our heart and to walk with him wherever we go.

Abiding in awe-filled attention drew Thérèse to bear with joy the weight of the crosses Christ asked her to carry. She knew that she was in the presence of a mystery she might never fathom, but what did that matter when, in her words, everything is grace. High above us as God may be, God is also nearer to us than we are to ourselves.

At such moments of awe, faith takes us where rational analysis alone cannot go. Even the words of a poet and storyteller like Thérèse fall short of the reality she experienced. We, too, are left stammering with a vocabulary reduced to one word: *Yes.* Your will, not mine be done. In the wake of such faith, we let go of the baggage we used to carry, admitting without any apology this plain truth: "Not that we are competent of ourselves to claim anything as coming from us; our competence is from God, who has made us competent to be ministers of a new covenant, not of letter but of spirit; for the letter kills, but the Spirit gives life" (2 Cor 3:5–6). Neither pain nor pleasure, failure nor success, illness nor health could cause us to end our walk. The words of Jesus are sufficient to guide us through the stormiest of nights since "perfect love casts out fear" (1 Jn 4:18).

Such love is like a magnet that attracts to itself many other virtues, including confidence in the Divine Plan behind every change we must undergo. Accompanying us is the Lord's assurance that he is the Good Shepherd, who will lead us home. Reading the life of Saint Benedict proves that the blessings of remaining in Christ are undeniable. St. Augustine of Hippo trusted enough to put on the Lord Jesus Christ and undergo radical conversion. St. Teresa of Ávila reformed the Carmelite Order. St. Maximilian Kolbe chose starvation in a Nazi bunker to save another prisoner's life. St. Maria Faustina Kowalska prayed, "Jesus, I trust in you," because she knew that he would give her the grace she needed to fulfill every command, however narrow the way on which he asked her to walk.

The call to holiness, wholeness, and happiness is universal. This general call then becomes specific in different kinds of vocations (marital, single, religious, clerical), while our avocations might involve being a teacher, business executive, artist, nurse, physician, scholar, chef, or a mixture of any of these. All three aspects of our life call — the universal, the vocational, and the avocational — harmonize us inwardly with Christ and help us outwardly to be more compassionate and competent disciples, who offer care to a wounded world in Christ's name. The Advocate sent to us by Jesus (see Jn 15:26), the Holy Spirit, travels with us on this journey of prayer and practice.

Our vocational choice, along with the avocational choices that accompany it, embody our calling in Christ. Vocations, as well as avocations, may change over the course of a lifetime in accordance with our providential destiny. A married person may become a widow. An accountant may go to graduate school and become a professor of economics. A retired pastor may enter a chaplaincy program. In all cases, the guiding light behind these transitions, their chief characteristic, is our willingness to follow the narrow way in fidelity to our life's call in the Lord.

We begin to see that the guidance of God is not like a hotline from the Spirit in heaven to us on earth; instead, his guidance hides in the changeless and changing demands that accompany the vocational and avocational expressions of our true calling. For example, a teacher may have to counsel a distraught student.

A social worker may need to spend time in a shelter to understand the plight of homeless persons. Day after day, we respond prudently to those in need of our assistance.

Abiding with Jesus in a person-to-Person relationship is the surest means of finding and following the directives for discipleship he decrees for us. He appoints wise, learned, and experienced walkers on the way to help us fulfill our God-guided destiny without being troubled or afraid (see Jn 14:27). The one directive all agree upon is that growth in the life of the Spirit entails dying to selfishness and surrendering our life wholly into God's hands.

Sustaining this dynamic of spiritual direction is formative reading of Holy Scripture and the writings of the spiritual masters. With the docility of true disciples, we dwell meditatively on what evokes our response to God's call. We do not grasp avidly for new knowledge; rather we submit to legitimate authority and seek to appropriate the truth spoken by the Author of Life in every facet of our inner and relational field of formation.

Abiding by Directives of Discipleship

"Cast all your anxiety on him, because he cares for you" (1 Pt 5:7). To cast all our cares on Jesus is a deeply consoling directive. When our turn onto the narrow way evokes anxiety, now is not the time to try to solve our problems on our own but to rely on the Lord. Such trust signifies intimacy between friends, who know one another through and through, who follow the same road, and who anticipate their needs before either one of them asks for help.

Christ goes ahead of us to prepare a place in heaven for us. This is a powerful directive of discipleship by which we ought to abide. We are precious in his sight; we are the apple of his eye (see Dt 32:10); we are cared for by him every step of the way. As our sense of direction gains in clarity, so does our ability to say *yes* to the gift that we are. Our ability to meet the demands of everyday situations without disrespecting our own and others' gifts also gains effectiveness. We maintain a caring presence in the midst of trying moments as well as during the routines of the day. We remain patient and flexible in our interactions with others and show by example the lasting fruits of living in time as if we were already in eternity. Remembering that we are only humble instruments called to serve the Lord and to draw others to him brings into focus our goal of going through the narrow gate to go heavenward.

Once an elderly priest, renowned for his gifts of direction, paused after Mass to ponder a parishioner's question: "How do you know when you're coming closer go God?" He smiled and replied, "You know it when you're doing God's will. You just know it." His answer came without hesitation and with the confidence of a lifetime of experience. He did not stop and think, nor did he enter into a lengthy discussion. He just knew what it meant to live the truth told to us by no less a legitimate authority than the apostle James: "Draw near to God, and he will draw near to you" (Jas 4:8).

Aligning Our Life with Gospel Values

Consider the Gospel passage, "Sell all that you own and distribute the money to the poor, and you will have a treasure in heaven; then come, follow me" (Lk 18:22). For one person, "all that you own" might mean time or talent; for another, possessions; for still another, prejudiced attitudes that kept him or her closed off from others. Likewise, "the poor" does not always mean the materially destitute. Aren't we all poor due to original sin and the need for redemption? Is it not imperative that we align our lives with gospel values that mirror the caring presence of Christ in our personhood and in the world at large? Whatever our vocation may be, the Lord solemnly tells us: "Amen, I say to you, whatever you did for one of these least brothers [and sisters] of mine, you did for me" (Mt 25:40, NABRE).

What we do is not merely a burden to be borne but a sacred duty that binds together our productive *I* and our caring *I*. With the help of grace, we feel released from the immature urge to match our worth to what we accomplish. We allow *kairos* time to pierce through *chronos* so that on the narrow way we find how to give eternal meaning to our time-bound obligations and concerns.

Instead of computing hours in terms of future tasks and profits, we dwell in the timelessness of useless presence that lets us be with the Lord. This gaze upon the face of God is an act of faith beyond comprehension, yet it enables us to conform our lives to Christ's and radiate his likeness to others. From the ground of contemplation, we go forth to act as Jesus would in the world. We want those we love and serve not to see us, but to see the Lord in us. We stand ready, willing, and able to obey the directives of discipleship we receive. For reasons yet to be revealed, we may be able to do nothing more than to relinquish our quest for sanctity and service into his wounded and transfigured hands while we pray:

Lord,
You read my heart, you see the secrets of my life,
my lostness in lust and little things, not harmonized
in loving worship of you alone, my Lord.
O let me be within your loving spotless Son
a worshipper in spirit and in truth,
a candle burning brightly for the Lord.
Turn my days into a joyful celebration
of the mystery that is my origin and end.
Unite me with you, high priest of humanity.

Alpha and Omega, beginning and end,
firstborn of all creatures.
For you have chosen me
before the foundation of the world,
you are the vibration of my soul.
Make me a caring presence in the universe,
blending all creatures inwardly
into a song of praise and adoration.
Let the radiance of my worship of you
shine upon my daily doings.
Change the world before my inner eye
into a revelation of your splendor.
Shining forth most brightly,
the destiny of all that is.

Pause and Ponder

- With what companion or guide would I want to walk on the narrow way? Why would I trust their advice concerning what advances and what deters my progress?
- If certain time-bound concerns prevent me from abiding by the directives of discipleship, am I willing to cut these ties so that I can travel more lightly?

STEP FOUR
Embrace Suffering for Christ's Sake

Overcoming Perdition and Being Transformed

*I delight in the way of your decrees
as much as in all riches.*

Psalm 119:14

We cannot enter through the narrow gate to transformation unless we are willing to embrace the cross. Saint Benedict urges us in the fourth step of the ladder of humility to trust in the meaning of life's crosses and to practice patient endurance.

When Corrie ten Boom and her sister Betsie were sent to the concentration camp at Ravensbruck, the lovely life they knew in their father's watchmaking shop in Haarlem ended. Now they were subject to the narrowest corridors of humiliation, star-vation, and persecution, to the point of death. What did they do? They ministered to those in prison with the words of hope they found in their cherished Bible. They gave women suffer-ing from every form of deprivation access to God's saving word. The blacker the night around them grew, the brighter and more beautiful burned the promises of God. The sisters had no way of knowing that God wove their story into the fabric of a provi-dential plan to destroy the evils of Nazism and lead the world to liberation from the perdition caused by this reign of terror.

As we read in Proverbs 3:5–6, "Trust in the LORD with all your heart, / and do not rely on your own insight. / In all your ways acknowledge him, / and he will make straight your paths." Such trust, let's face it, is a tall order. It means holding tight to the con-viction that love will triumph over hate; peace over war; faith over doubt. Perhaps the proverb says to trust with all our heart because by means of mere logic alone, it would be hard to conclude that life will go on after death; that the cross is the way of salvation; that the exalted will be humbled and the humble exalted.

This heart-knowledge is God's gift to us. It steers us away from choosing unwisely to rely on our own understanding. The "wasps" of "why" and "what if" will sting us mercilessly if we torture ourselves by demanding answers to unanswerable ques-tions rather than bowing in awe before the mystery at the center of everything. Our role is that of an obedient servant open to the directing power of divine grace. It is not for us to lead on the narrow way, but to match our steps to those of the Master. When storms approach, whether gradual or sudden, predictable or un-predictable, we find a wayside station and shelter there. We wait upon the Lord and only then do we resume our walk.

In cooperation with grace, Corrie and Betsie ten Boom ac-cepted that they were messengers of a mystery greater than ei-ther of them. With the depth of faith that moves mountains, they saw the meaning behind the hardships inflicted upon them. God gave them the grace to rise from the grip of evil to the glory of evangelization.

Our story echoes theirs each time we move closer to Christ on the narrow way. The light of truth radiating from the word of God lets us see who we are as disciples of our Divine Master. The persecution that accompanies our witness to the truth is in the end of no consequence to us, for "who will separate us from the love of Christ? Will hardship, or distress, or persecution, or famine, or nakedness, or peril, or sword? ... No, in all these things we are more than conquerors through him who loved us. For I am convinced that neither death, nor life, nor angels, nor rulers, nor things present, nor things to come, nor powers, nor height, nor depth, nor anything else in all creation, will be able to separate us from the love of God in Christ Jesus our Lord" (Rom 8:35–39).

Embrace Suffering in and with the Lord

Whereas the wide road deflects us from seeking the meaning of life's challenges, the narrow way influences our appraisals of what we ought to do, no matter the sacrifices it entails. The holy ones of God embrace the challenges posed by crosses in and with the Lord; they remind us that we are in danger of losing our way unless we turn to Christ and say with the apostle Paul, "May I never boast of anything except the cross ... by which the world has been crucified to me, and I to the world" (Gal 6:14).

Every event in life, from the birth of a child to the death of a parent, entails some suffering. Every encounter, from a passing meeting with a friend that ends far too soon, to the enforced solitude impinged upon everyone under the burden of a global pandemic, is a chapter in the unfolding story of how to walk the narrow way and refuse to reverse our course.

None of us knows in advance how the pieces of the puzzle

of life will fall into place. Who of us is capable of penetrating the meaning of salvation history? All we can do is cling fast to the Lord and attend to his beckoning, knowing that we never walk alone. Our understanding may be too limited to grasp all but the small step in front of us. Rather than trying to analyze what awaits us, it is enough to live in faith. The Holy Spirit never fails to guide us from the Calvary moments of life to the glory of Easter morn.

Ours is not an in and out, up and down, occasional story of belief, but the "assurance of things hoped for, the conviction of things not seen" (Heb 11:1). Our faith in the meaning of suffering is a gift that keeps on giving the more we ruminate on the life of Christ and cling to him as our dearest companion on the narrow way. At the most unexpected moments, faith provides evidence that the Eternal does pierce through the temporal, and that the finite is only a breath away from the Infinite. Faith of this depth will always be life-changing; it is the key that unlocks every conversion experience and gives us the courage to witness to the Word in the throes of agony and uplifts of ecstasy.

There will be times on our walk with Jesus when we feel overtaken by waves of exhaustion. The Tempter knows when this happens and goes on the attack. Our strongest ally at such indecisive moments is Holy Scripture. Its promises inspire us; its teachings inform us. Exemplary are these memorable words from the prophet Ezekiel: "A new heart I will give you, and a new spirit I will put within you; and I will remove from your body the heart of stone and give you a heart of flesh. I will put my spirit within you, and make you follow my statues and be careful to observe my ordinances. Then you shall live in the land that I gave to your ancestors; and you shall be my people, and I will be your God" (Ez 36:26–28).

Without the grace of receiving a new heart, we may carry

in our chest a weight that drains our energy and renders life a living hell. We need God's steady hand on our shoulders to shake us loose from shackles of disobedience and redirect our steps homeward to heaven. Now is the time to pause, take a deep breath, and assess where our heart is — with God or lost in useless worry?

We may secretly wish that God had made us in a more robotic way, without free will and the necessity of having to choose good over evil. Yet that dehumanized stance was not God's intention.

Mary chose to say *"fiat"* — your will not mine be done — when she consented to be the mother of our Lord (see Lk 1:38).

Joseph could have ignored the angel's warning and stayed in Bethlehem, but he made the courageous choice to flee to Egypt with Mary and Jesus to escape the wrath of Herod (see Mt 2:13–15).

Jesus rejected Peter's outcry that he not go to Jerusalem, calling him Satan, and reminding him what the choice to obey the Father's will really means: "You are a stumbling block to me; for you are setting your mind not on divine things but on human things" (Mt 16:23).

One tried and true way to stay focused on this teaching is to purify our minds of self-centered passions and purposes that cause us to distrust God's providence and expose us to any number of stumbling blocks, from anxious needs to overdependent demands.

Overcome Perdition

To avoid the broad road that leads to destruction of our inner and relational life, we must pledge never to violate the God-given integrity of self and others. The following pointers help us bypass the temptation to choose the path of perdition, showing us instead ways of loving that are freeing, not forced; compassionate, not coercive:

- Be mindful of what brings healing in body, mind, and spirit to ourselves and others.
- Be patient with our personal struggles and empathize with what others have to endure.
- Cease being so judgmental of human faults and failings and submit them to God's forgiveness.
- Create around us an atmosphere that encourages trust in the Lord and rely on his power in us to convert our hearts.

At times we know with surprising clarity what God asks of us. At other times we may only catch glimpses of this or that facet of the struggle between obedience and rebellion. In either case, we are free to walk the narrow way and, should we detour from it for whatever reason, we can seek the light once more and shun the perils that overwhelm us.

Whenever we come to another fork in the road, our task is to choose the way that leads to Christ-like love and labor, knowing that "we have done only what we ought to have done!" (Lk 17:10).

Be Transformed

Such a thoughtful approach to life offers us more than facile solutions to passing needs; it signifies our transformation "from one degree of glory to another; for this comes from the Lord, the Spirit" (2 Cor 3:18). Action, complemented by reflection, helps us to find the best way to participate in the life of Christ and to dedicate ourselves to the evangelization of all nations in his name.

Knowing that we are searchers, pilgrims, and sojourners on the way, unpredictability no longer frightens us. God's promise of transformation loosens us from those things we may have glued our hopes upon and helps us to live each day in anticipation of eternity.

Daily happenings become the windows through which we behold, in light and shadow, the unconditional love that embraces and directs our life. Upon reflection, we see providential patterns not previously recognized but now revealed with new clarity. We catch the threads that weave together the whole tapestry of what has been, what is, and what will come. We listen, as the apostle Paul tells us, to a mystery! "We will not all die, but we will all be changed, in a moment, in the twinkling of an eye, at the last trumpet. For the trumpet will sound, and the dead will be raised imperishable, and will be changed" (1 Cor 15:51–52). In trying to describe this mysterious passage from time to eternity, no words suffice, and so we pray:

> Lord,
> Do not mask the mystery
> that imprints itself on human hearts.
> Do not depart or paralyze the potency
> in me to be an epiphanic plea,
> a lighthouse in a stormy sea.
>
> Help me not to surrender to the press of busyness,
> to anxious control, to hunger for success.
> Mirror in me the Mystery of love and gentleness.
>
> In the midst of human history,
> grant me the grace to be
> a lasting story of God's glory,
> revealing the nobility
> of each pilgrim journeying on earth
> while enfleshing the eternal, everlasting dream.

Pause and Ponder

- How does walking on the narrow way enable me to see more clearly why I ought to embrace suffering for Christ's sake and share my joy with everyone I meet?
- Have I experienced my need to overcome perdition in order to grow in perfect trust of the Lord and be transformed in him?

Part Two

Choose the Hard Road

*Blessed be the God and Father of our Lord Jesus Christ,
the Father of mercies and the God of all consolation,
who consoles us in all our affliction, so that we may be
able to console those who are in any affliction with the
consolation with which we ourselves are consoled by God.
For just as the sufferings of Christ are abundant for us,
so also our consolation is abundant through Christ. If we
are being afflicted, it is for your consolation and salvation;
if we are being consoled, it is for your consolation,
which you experience when you patiently endure the same
sufferings that we are also suffering. Our hope for you is
unshaken; for we know that as you share in our sufferings,
so also you share in our consolation.*

2 Corinthians 1:3–7

STEP FIVE
Confess All Faults and Weaknesses

Avoiding Hindrances to Living with Christ

I will meditate on your precepts,
and fix my eyes on your ways.

Psalm 119:15

A familiar slogan reads: Bloom where you are planted. Wherever we are, in family rooms or business offices, wearing a white collar or blue, we need to avoid any and all hindrances to living with Christ. If we give children the loving guidance they deserve, then we bloom as teachers and parents. If we are patient with annoying people, no matter how aggravated we feel, then we bloom as the kind and courteous Christians we profess to be.

To foster in ourselves and others this kind of blooming, we need to know the difference between what deadens our spirit and what draws us to new life. According to Saint Benedict, the fifth step on the ladder of humility counsels us to confess our faults and weaknesses and seek reconciliation with God, mindful always of the depth of Divine Mercy. He confirms our belief that "living is Christ and dying [to selfishness, corruption, and dishonesty] is gain" (Phil 1:21). Relying on the forgiveness of God is what enables us to cultivate compunction of heart and confess our faults and failings.

To choose the hard road is not a question of having the brawny strength that builds muscles, but the inner strength and moral fiber that builds character. Hindrances to living with Christ fall by the wayside when we do what he asks of us. We habitually make sound decisions and confess when we are not in touch with God's will. The temptation to go along with the demands of vocal crowds, without paying attention to our personal calling, lessens in intensity.

The narrow way encourages interaction with our surroundings, whereas the road to perdition inclines us to interpret daily interactions in an often unjust and uncharitable manner. It presents us with a variety of options for living in, with, and through Christ instead of losing hope and blaming others for causing our problems. We do not allow the business of the day to become so all-consuming that we overlook the challenge to do what Christ would do in our situation. We see others not as pawns on a chessboard we can manipulate, but as people of God, infinitely worthy of respect. Yesterday we may have cared for an elderly member of our family. Today we leave work early to shop and prepare dinner for old friends. Tomorrow we need to set aside time to converse with a colleague about how to resolve a tense relationship at work.

Once we may have attended to these everyday occurrences in a more or less routine fashion; now we see them as occasions to walk the narrow way with Christ at our side. Our lives are more aligned with his. At our aged relative's bedside, it is his hand that holds hers. We picture him as the chief guest at our table, offering pleasant greetings and warm hospitality to everyone seated there. We let go of our preconceived agendas and thank God for the beauty of life from youth to old age, and for providing creative solutions to what could have resulted in cold-hearted encounters.

Rather than retreating to warring camps, we agree that it is better to engage in common-sense dialogue. We see how foolish it is to puff up with pride and block the flow of self-giving love. We reject what hinders this grace and accept what promotes conformity to Christ at this and future junctures of our faith journey.

Confessing Our Resistance to Listening to Christ

Everything from ingrained prejudices to habitual disobedience, from jealousy to harsh judgmentalism, may weaken our capacity to accept Christ's invitation to choose the hard road. The firmer our choice for the narrow way, the less likely we are to listen to voices bent on swaying us with untruths contrary to the word of the Lord. Even on the most miserable of days, we do our best to focus on gospel teachings and to hear them with the inner ears of our heart.

Concern over what has been or curiosity about what will be is less important to us than remaining present to Christ here and now. He wants us to face reality, not fantasize about a less narrow way to follow. Trust and surrender lessen the danger of losing our way. We prefer to set in motion plans and projects rooted in the wisdom of our faith and not in subtle or overt violations of the demands of discipleship.

Such listening relieves us from the dominance of destructive egoism; it instills in us the courage to confess our faults and seek the grace of reconciling friendship with our Lord.

In the words of Proverbs 16:18, "Pride goes before destruction, and a haughty spirit before a fall." When we assume that control is in our hands, we risk taking a detour that despoils our living with Christ. We forget that God's ways are infinitely superior to our own. Our goal must be to relinquish selfish demands and grow in the grace of self-denying surrender: "Thus says the LORD: / Stand at the crossroads, and look, / and ask for the ancient paths, / where the good way lies; and walk in it, / and find rest for your souls" (Jer 6:16).

Avoiding the Danger of Ego-Exaltation

Only when we silence the clamor of ego-exaltation can we proclaim with the apostle Paul, "I can do all things through [Christ] who strengthens me" (Phil 4:13). I, on my own, can do nothing without the help of God. This is the opposite of ego-exaltation, which declares that I alone, by means of my own power, can do anything I set my mind to accomplish.

On the narrow way, we reject the myth of self-sufficiency. Surrender to God's will, often in the face of disappointment and failure, becomes second nature to us. Pleasant or unpleasant challenges, exciting or routine demands, consolations or desolations do not disturb our equanimity. We catch ourselves when we become too tense and hurried or too lax and unresponsive to what Christ would have us do. To see the world from his perspective is to welcome with equal fervor life's peaks and valleys, its times of victory and defeat.

Of this we can be sure: Entering through the narrow gate makes it easier for us to discern the anxious tension and useless worry that accompany ego-exaltation. Our first choice is to beg God for the grace to overcome these hindrances and to enhance our capacity for reflective living. We prefer to hope against hope and to love without always expecting love in return.

Seeing Divine Directives in Every Situation

Imagine what it would have been like to be Saul before he fulfilled his call to be Paul. In every way Saul exemplified the path to destruction. He was a Pharisee from Tarsus, at enmity with the Christian community. So antagonistic was his behavior that he approved the stoning of Stephen and allowed his killers to lay their coats at his feet (see Acts 7:58 and 8:1).

Saul ravaged the church "by entering house after house; dragging off both men and women" and committing them to prison (Acts 8:3). He seemed the least likely person for God to snatch from the trap of perdition and lead to the freedom of life in Christ. Yet this was his destiny. The Savior himself put him on the narrow way, not when he was praying for conversion, but when he was "still breathing threats and murder against the disciples of the Lord" (Acts 9:1).

Saul sought the counsel of the High Priest to get permission to locate anyone "who belonged to the Way, men or women, [that] he might bring them bound to Jerusalem" (Acts 9:2). His bellicose plan imploded, thanks to a stunning example of Divine intervention.

Every Christian knows Saul's conversion story. His whole life changed the moment he fell to the ground, surrounded by a flashing light from heaven, and heard the Lord ask why he had chosen to persecute him. When Saul questioned whose voice this was, he received the awesome reply: "I am Jesus" (Acts 9:5). Instructed regarding what to do, Saul, now blinded by the light, followed his new Master's orders, received baptism from Ananias, a devout believer, and in due time acquired a new name. The way Paul would follow brought light to the Gentiles and seeded the evangelization of the world.

To make him a follower of Christ, God stripped Paul of his arrogance through imprisonments and countless floggings. He reports:

> Five times I have received from the Jews the forty lashes minus one. Three times I was beaten with rods. Once I received a stoning. Three times I was shipwrecked; for a night and a day I was adrift at sea; on frequent journeys, in danger from rivers, danger from bandits, danger from my own people, danger from Gentiles, danger in the city, danger in the wilderness, danger at sea, danger from false brothers and sisters; in toil and hardship, through many a sleepless night, hungry and thirsty, often without food, cold and naked. (2 Corinthians 11:24–27)

Given such ordeals, is it any wonder mere mortals like us might balk at the invitation to adhere to the narrow way?

Paul softens our fear when he boasts of his inadequacy and reminds us of what the Lord told him: "My grace is sufficient for you, for power is made perfect in weakness" (2 Cor 12:9). He reaches the conclusion every follower of Christ must take to heart: "Therefore I am content with weaknesses, insults, hardships, persecutions, and calamities for the sake of Christ; for whenever I am weak, then I am strong" (2 Cor 12:10).

We learn from Paul's experience that suffering the cross prepares us to enter into solidarity with every Christian who has ever walked on the narrow way. We cannot fulfill any Christ-formed, gospel-directed, Church-oriented call without the courage to accept persecution and misunderstanding, however frequently we experience these crosses.

At times we must fight to overcome the evils in society and the oppressive structures that promote injustice, war, and persecution. We combat the sinful behaviors manifested in under-privileged neighborhoods; in unjustly distributed medical care; in the promotion of the wrong kind of nourishment for young children; in institutional violence, pornography, global conflict, human trafficking, and drug addiction.

We may promote corrective actions in various forms of ministry, knowing all the while that without prayer, no healing of a lasting nature will ever happen. The more active a role we play in spreading the Gospel, the more contemplative we need to become. What we do from nonviolent resistance to exposing the evils of corrupt regimes depends on who Christ calls us to be. No matter what we accomplish, we must pray for the grace to incarnate our call in fidelity to God's plan for our life.

Paul's words leave no room for ambiguity in this regard: "Do not be conformed to this world, but be transformed by the renewing of your minds, so that you may discern what is the will of God — what is good and acceptable and perfect" (Rom 12:2). Embedded in this imperative is a clear picture of just how narrow the way of interior renewal is. Unless we renew our minds, we cannot change our hearts and discern the will of God.

The obstacles strewn on our path are formidable. The world allures us to attach our star to pleasures and possessions, to live as if there were no tomorrow. We put on hold the decisions, outlooks, and attitudes we must acquire if we want to enjoy the freedom of transformation in Christ. What path will we follow? What consequences accompany our choice? What drains our energy? What replenishes it? We must deal with these questions when we walk on the razor's edge that is the narrow way, and so we pray:

Lord,
Fill me with your words,

those shining bridges
that like rainbows
harmonize my doings
with the heaven of your presence.
Let them penetrate my busy mind,
my dried up soul,
like fragrant oil.
If you grant me a fleeting sense
of your abiding,
let me not clutch it greedily,
but flow gently with the mystery
of your appearance and departure
in my daily life.

Pause and Ponder

- Am I honest enough to identify and confess those parts of my existence that are more self-centered than Christ-centered? What are they and what must I do to correct my course?
- Having found that the narrow way is not that narrow after all, how has walking its length and breadth increased my capacity to love others as Jesus loves me?

STEP SIX
Be Content to Be
Poor Servants

Enjoying the Peace of Discipleship

Put false ways far from me;
and graciously teach me your law.

Psalm 119:29

The sixth step in Chapter Seven of Saint Benedict's *Rule* expresses the humble awareness that however much we have done in our life, we are still unworthy servants, content to take the lowest place and loath to call attention to ourselves. We are disciples of Jesus, our Master. To serve him in the most menial of circumstances fills us with peace and draws us to the depths of discipleship.

Peace is not a static condition, nor is it a state of apathy or placid indifference; it is a dynamic quest for harmony in our

73

hearts and in our world. The peace we seek finds its source in the Prince of Peace (see Is 9:6), who bestowed on us as his farewell gift (see Jn 14:27) "the peace of God, which surpasses all understanding" (Phil 4:7).

Such peace goes beyond temporary euphoria and becomes over time a permanent state of being, which finds support in the awesome hope that one day "the wolf shall live with the lamb, / the leopard shall lie down with the kid, / the calf and the lion and the fatling together, / and a little child shall lead them" (Is 11:6).

Under this canopy of peace, we experience the blessed assurance of our being cared for by God, both in adversity and prosperity. We recognize more readily the obstacles that threaten this peace, from temporary impatience and grumbling when we do not get our way, to heart-pounding episodes of senseless violence. So intent may we be on solving our own problems that we slip into somber, non-communicative moods that dispel any semblance of harmony between us.

When we listen to life as an invitation to poverty of spirit and inner peace, we begin to enjoy the consolations of discipleship Christ promised us. Every event, from putting meals on the table to sitting in meditation, offers us the opportunity to be as calm and quiet as a weaned child on its mother's lap (see Ps 131:2). A loaf of bread, a glass of wine, a friendly face, an awesome storm, a radiant rainbow — all evoke appreciation for every peaceful disclosure of God's presence in our lives from birth to death.

Br. Lawrence of the Resurrection (1611–1691) was a saintly Carmelite lay brother, who taught devotion to the practice of the presence of God and the peace it grants. Before deciding in middle age to enter the Discalced Carmelite order, he served in the army and worked as a household employee. This calling continued in religious life, where he remained a humble worker, cooking and cleaning the kitchen and performing cobbler tasks for the duration of his life. Recognized as a spiritual guide by religious and laity alike, this simple friar lived an exemplary life and died a holy death at the age of eighty.

After Brother Lawrence's death, Abbé Joseph de Beaufort, who had visited him on a regular basis, published a memoir based on their conversations, together with sixteen of Brother Lawrence's letters. In these writings we learn the secret of a peaceful life on the way of perfection: being with Jesus in the midst of everyday events.

Brother Lawrence believed that what conforms us to Christ is not learned treatises or mystical visions, but a heart resolutely turned to him and to service of others for his sake. Christ-centered love enables us to reform the pockets of pride still lurking within us and to live our commitments with the peace and joy of Jesus, rather than with an endless litany of complaints. Brother Lawrence cautions us to reject living in stale, tedious, and duty-bound austerity that can never be inspiring to others. How can we practice the presence of God if we feel chained to our daily routines like felons "doing time"?

Living on this insensitive treadmill puts us at risk of drifting far from the narrow way and failing to renew our awareness of what Christ would say or do if he were walking with us. Life will always be less perfect than we expected, but these imperfections provide the opportunity we need to grow in fidelity. Instead of causing us to lose confidence in the efficacy of our call, these limits bless us by reminding us of just how dependent we are on the grace of God.

Rather than trying to control everyone around us, we pray for the peace to be free from willful plans and projects so that we can recover our sense of Christ's presence and renew our reasons for following him. We look at the pots and pans of daily life with a fresh eye, penetrating below their surface appearance to the hidden depths of their sacred meaning.

This way of being changes our outlook on the world and

reveals the temporal as a pointer to the Eternal. Yesterday we extended a helping hand to a blind person crossing the street. Today we offer our seat on the rush-hour bus to an elderly lady. Tomorrow we befriend a frail child on the sidelines of the soccer team. These kinds of encounters are life-giving. They enable us to see one another as members of the Mystical Body of Christ, as participants in the life of the Trinity, as a community of sinners invited to become part of the communion of saints.

Cultivating and Curtailing the Practice of Peace

To share the peace of Jesus, we have to detach ourselves from what is less than God. Nothing less than God can quell the restlessness of our heart. Rest comes when we refuse to adopt the false peace a world without God promises. We can know the difference between true and false peace, because illusory peace vanishes like a withering bouquet, while true peace has staying power.

The Sermon on the Mount offers counsels that help us to cultivate the practice of peace. The blessings and promises Jesus proclaims chart the way of discipleship he calls us to pursue:

- "Blessed are the poor in spirit, for theirs is the kingdom of heaven" (Mt 5:3). The first step to lasting peace is to depend on God for everything.
- "Blessed are those who mourn, for they will be comforted" (Mt 5:4). A second key to peace is to attend to God's loving and allowing will, especially in times of suffering.
- "Blessed are the meek, for they will inherit the earth" (Mt 5:5). Peace fosters the virtues of docility and humility, both of which honor Jesus as the model of our search for truth.
- "Blessed are those who hunger and thirst for righteousness, for they will be filled" (Mt 5:6). Peaceful

persons choose sanctity and service as two sources
of lasting fulfillment.

- "Blessed are the merciful, for they will receive mercy" (Mt 5:7). To exude compassion for one another
  and to grow in mutual care and concern always lead
  us to inner peace.
- "Blessed are the pure in heart, for they will see God"
  (Mt 5:8). To love the people of God, with no strings
  attached, is an ideal opening to peaceful relationships.
- "Blessed are the peacemakers, for they will be called
  children of God" (Mt 5:9). To live in peace and to
  share this divine gift with others is a sure sign of
  mature discipleship.
- "Blessed are those who are persecuted for righteousness' sake, for theirs is the kingdom of heaven" (Mt
  5:10). When we walk the way of the cross and forgive
  our foes, we become peacekeepers wherever we are.

To live the beatitudes alters our concept of what constitutes the
practice of peace. True peace lasts even when others persecute
and misunderstand us. Detractors falsely accused Jesus himself
of wrongdoing, yet he made peace his farewell gift.

What may astound us is that not even onslaughts of slan-
derous gossip can destroy our peace. In particularly painful moments, we remember that heaven awaits us when our pilgrimage
through life comes to a close. Our suffering is as nothing com-
pared to the joy that will be ours.

In the Sermon on the Mount and throughout Sacred Scripture, we receive messages directed to us personally and to the
community of faith that reveal many good reasons to follow the
narrow way. Consider these words from the Book of Revelation:
"Be earnest, therefore, and repent. Listen! I am standing at the

door, knocking; if you hear my voice and open the door, I will come in to you and eat with you, and you with me" (Rv 3:19–20). Here are three imperatives to enhance our intimacy with the Lord and to experience the consolations of discipleship:

- *Be earnest.* To do so with confidence, we must let God form us through what we read so that, with all the saints, God can make us zealous instruments to form others.
- *Repent.* To live a life worthy of friendship with the Lord, we must experience daily compunction of heart. However dense the obstacles strewn on our path may be, we must avail ourselves of the grace of repentance needed to remove them. We have to train ourselves to meet the challenges posed by the narrow way and not grow discouraged. In the face of whatever confronts us, we must have the courage to seek forgiveness and go forward.
- *Listen.* Faith depends on our listening to the Lord and heeding his call. Those of us with eyes to see and ears to hear know what it means to be "salt of the earth" (Mt 5:13) and "light of the world" (Mt 5:14). The Lord knocks at the door of our heart. Are we ready to let him enter this sacred chamber and break bread with us?

Each of these imperatives complements the many counsels we receive on the way to becoming worthy disciples of Jesus. Rather than assume a joyless "savior complex," we keep before our mind's eye our commitment to radiate Christ's love and to let others glimpse its light in our whole being. We take time to be in the presence of Jesus, rather than obsessing on the business of doing. We do our best to discard the anxiety we used to feel when we failed to perform with super-efficiency. Reserving time for formative reading and meditative reflection gives us the peace of mind to avoid self-castigation and to respond as fully as possible to the Lord when he knocks at our door.

We often desire to identify our worth in God's eyes with the number of tasks we perform. Time urgency destroys our peace. Measurable accomplishments become far more important than resting with Jesus, which we may even begin to see as a waste of time!

The more we turn our attention to the Master, the more likely we are to live the paradox that "all who exalt themselves will be humbled, and those who humble themselves will be exalted" (Lk 14:11). In addition to neither grumbling about occasional ill treatment nor blaming others for our mistakes, we maintain a gracious heart and show respect for our sisters and brothers. We celebrate the creative potential in every person rather than reducing them to a "see one, see them all" perspective that veils their uniqueness.

Every time we disconnect our inmost calling to mirror the peace of Jesus from managing the demands of daily life, we risk veering onto the path of perdition and failing to practice the presence of God. Lack of listening encourages blind conformity to political correctness. We prefer polls, labels, and slogans to the challenging task of cherishing originality and never reducing our faith to a collection of routine religious practices.

Living as Poor Servants at Peace with Others and the Lord

All of us need the peace that healed our broken world that starry night in Bethlehem when angelic hosts sang, "Glory to God in the highest heaven, and on earth peace among those whom he favors" (Lk 2:14).

To live in peace with the Lord in the spirit of servanthood leads to a life of virtue. We temper our tendency to speak harshly to wounded souls and acknowledge in humility our own and others' need for compassion. We avoid as a rule the devastating effects of destructive cynicism, sly sarcasm, and haughty condescension and try to put an end to such behaviors once and for all. We ponder how we can thank Jesus for the gifts of peace and joy he gives us to share with others.

Contrast these virtues to the vices of violence, ill will, and hatred that ravage our world. Only the presence of Jesus in our midst can grant us relief from every form of cruelty and renew our hope in the innate goodness of humankind.

The mask of impatient, uncaring self-sufficiency hides countless souls that are longing for peace. It is tempting to be cold and indifferent to people scarred by sin and torn apart by its consequences, but such is not the way of discipleship. Our place is not to judge others but to grow in empathy for their suffering, and so we pray:

Let me dwell daily in your peace, my Lord.
Let it give gentle form to my unfolding.
Let me no longer be the lonely shepherd of my life.
Bring me home from the bracing highlands of the mind,
    from the dead-end streets in which I shiver in despair.
Shelter my soul tenderly when disappointment
    hems me in.
Do not allow my soul to grow ponderous and bleak,
    keep alive in me a glimmer of your joy,
    let no adversity deter my course,
    nor defeat my slow advance.
Put a spring in my step, a smile in my heart.
Let me spend this life lightheartedly.
Fill it with verve and inspiration.

Ploughing, we praise; sailing, we sing,
   to land on the shore
   that teems with your presence.

Pause and Ponder

- Why is it impossible to enter through the narrow gate unless we make peace with ourselves and others?
- Of all the lessons Jesus conveys in the Sermon on the Mount, which one speaks most personally to me at this time of my life?

STEP SEVEN
Put on the Mind of Christ

Walking with Him through Persecution and Misunderstanding

I have chosen the way of faithfulness;
I set your ordinances before me.

Psalm 119:30

"'For who has known the mind of the Lord so as to instruct him?' But we have the mind of Christ" (1 Cor 2:16). Saint Paul confirms this revelation when he says, "Let the same mind be in you that was in Christ Jesus" (Phil 2:5). That mindset marks our entrance through the narrow gate. What propels us forward is the undeniable truth that when all else passes away, his words last (see Mt 24:35).

In the seventh degree of humility, Saint Benedict continues his counsel that to imitate Christ in our decisions and actions is to shun the entrapments of arrogant self-centeredness. The best way to do so is to welcome the persecutions and misunderstandings that come our way when we walk with Jesus. Day by day we grow in humble dependence on God's providence. We feel that Jesus, standing at our side, protects and understands us. Narrow as the path may seem, we never walk alone.

In the early Church, people knew Christ's followers as those "who belonged to the Way" (Acts 9:2). This Way, as Saint Paul told to the believers in Corinth, was that of love (see 1 Cor 12:31). That is "the new and living way that he opened for us … [the way we are to] approach with a true heart in full assurance of faith, with our hearts sprinkled clean from an evil conscience and our bodies washed with pure water" (Heb 10:20–22).

This powerful metaphor points to why we must put on the mind of Christ and walk with him as our dearest companion. To proceed, we cannot "be conformed to this world." Instead, we must "be transformed by the renewing of [our] minds, so that [we] may discern what is the will of God — what is good and acceptable and perfect" (Rom 12:2). However lost we feel, Christ turns our steps toward home and guides us to heaven. The way may be narrow, but it is the road that leads to life (see Mt 7:14).

We can expect misgivings to arise, but instead of thinking of them as stumbling blocks, we can view them as chances to pass over to the way of perfection so that the mind of Christ may become our own.

Praying for Divine Guidance

To excel in Christ-centered living, we need as a rule to interpret obstacles as openings to rebirth and renewal. It is problematic to seek a quick fix to become holy or to engage in excessive mortifications that lack the perennial wisdom of moderation. One wrong turn may give us glowing feelings of heroic achievement; the other may foster extremes of austerity. In reality, such practices only condone our inclination to proud self-reliance.

When we try to imitate the styles and actions of saints and reformers indiscriminately, we forgo humility and promote self-centeredness. We venture on the paths they took without asking ourselves if they are truly ours. We embrace certain tenets of asceticism or mysticism compulsively or hysterically. We detour around or miss altogether the path of grace that is in harmony with God's direction of our life.

A truly Spirit-guided life lets us stand before God as we are, with no illusions left. Walking with Christ and embracing his cross cuts through the façade of individualistic pretenses that serve only to hide our own willfulness.

Thanks be to God, once we turn to Christ, we realize that perfectionism has no place in our relationships. God gives grace to us before we do anything to deserve it. When Christ is the center, character flaws like the illusion of self-sufficiency lose their hold on us. God sees through our sinfulness not to banish us from heaven but to see us through to new ways of forgiveness and friendship:

> Though the Lord may give you the bread of adversity
> and the water of affliction, yet your Teacher will not hide
> himself any more, but your eyes shall see your Teacher.
> And when you turn to the right or when you turn to
> the left, your ears shall hear a word behind you, saying,
> "This is the way; walk in it." (Isaiah 30:20–21)

Approaching God More Closely

Here is a question worthy of daily reflection: Do we know, love, and serve God in this life so that we may one day be with him in paradise? Our Lord reminds us that we can tell a good from a bad tree by the fruit it produces (see Mt 7:17–20). Growth in fidelity is difficult to measure. It may be relatively invisible until we see in retrospect that we are bearing more fruit than we realized.

The plant on our windowsill might look as if it is on its last leg, but as soon as we water it and move it into the sun, several new shoots begin to bud forth. Our plant grew, as do we, silently but noticeably by means of hidden processes we can facilitate but not control.

The more we try to put on the mind of Christ, the more aware we become of changes for the better in our relationship with Christ. Trust in the Lord replaces the twinges of distrust that used to tug at our heart. We begin to make our decisions against the backdrop of our companionship with him, which spurs on our progress on the narrow way. We avail ourselves more often of the wellspring from whence all goodness flows by allowing no manifestation of the mind of Christ to pass us by.

When we seek Jesus, we do not have to put on airs. We can be as open about our burdens as a child confessing faults to an understanding parent. We may feel ashamed about the bad things we have done, but we have no doubt that we shall receive the refreshment of reconciliation.

Christ gives us food for the journey both on days when we feel weary and when energy abounds. All that matters is that we come to him trusting that he will "make with [us] an everlasting covenant" (Is 55:3). God will never break the bond between himself and us as long as we lay our burdens at the feet of Jesus.

Standing still in his presence consoles us. Taking refreshment from a table filled with good fare renews us. We are ready to go where the Spirit leads us. This spiritual sustenance strengthens us and satisfies our deepest longings. We experience what it means to be still while still moving, to be listening with inner attention while attending outwardly to our work. We flow with the guiding wisdom of God while serving his reign on earth.

We learn to commingle a certain stillness and a sense of determination. The bumps and bangs of life are less likely to diminish our contentment and composure. We can stand in the presence of God without succumbing to the pressures of a busy world forgetful of what really counts. We can move with purpose and direction, even if those around us seem to flounder haplessly. Whatever comes, we identify with a spiritual guide like Saint Paul, who tells us boldly: "Indeed, this is our boast, the testimony of our conscience: we have behaved in the world with frankness and godly sincerity, not by earthly wisdom but by the grace of God" (2 Cor 1:12). Like the apostle to the Gentiles, we too want to be persons who claim God as our center and move forward on the narrow way with God as our guide.

Being Befriended by the Lord

Imagine what it must have felt like to the disciples when Christ elevated them from mere servanthood to the status of friendship by saying: "No one has greater love than this, to lay down one's life for one's friends. You are my friends if you do what I command you" (Jn 15:13–14). As Christ listened to what he heard from his Father, so his friends were to listen to him and love one another as he loved them.

A faithful friend is a rare treasure, beyond any price (see Sir 6:15). Even when his friend Peter betrayed him, Jesus healed the temporary rift between them by his gifts of unconditional love and forgiveness. Peter chose in the end to enter through the narrow gate and follow Jesus to death on a cross — a sure sign that his friendship with the Lord would lead to eternal life.

To help us stay on the narrow path, Jesus draws each of us beyond casual companionship to true intimacy. He allows us to know him rather than merely knowing about him. Servants may depart from their master to pursue another position, but not friends. They are with him through thick and thin.

Jesus spoke to countless listeners, but not all of them heard his words. He performed miracles, but some recipients never thanked him. Still, he laid down his life for them. The question is: Are we ready to put ours aside for him? Are we willing to die to our fears, needs, prejudices, and defenses, so that we can begin to grasp with Saint Paul "the breadth and length and height and depth, and to know the love of Christ that surpasses knowledge, so that [we] may be filled with all the fullness of God" (Eph 3:18–19)?

To discover how to grow with Christ over a lifetime, we need to be still enough to hear the divine harmony that plays beneath the seemingly disharmonious events of everyday life. We learn to be aware of him the more we develop the discipline of walking with Christ as our dearest companion. We refuse to behave like passengers on a speeding train, who never see the countryside but only a blur of brown and green outside their compartment window. The Lord's friendship grants us the gift of learning to love him and one another with no semblance of infidelity.

Dawn appears slowly on the horizon. It does not rush to reveal at once the brightness of the day. The light of dawn comes to us in soft hues that fill us with wonder. Does not an early morn touch us by the fragile lacework-quilt of dew strung from leaves and flowers? How many times have we missed these graced in-breaking moments? Often, we are too busy to notice the gift of the dawn, too preoccupied to attend to divine disclosures in the midst of everydayness.

A friend of mine shared her experience of becoming aware of God's inspiration. At first, these divine movements were too delicate for her to recognize, but as time passed she began to realize the guiding lights they carried for her life. She developed open eyes to the dawning, especially at her lowest ebbs of disap-

pointment. After the accumulation of several small enlighten-
ments had broken in upon her, she began to see what God had
intended for her from the start. From that moment until now,
she has never ceased to marvel at the way God directs her life.
She has to be still and listen, but she knows that divine guidance
will come.

"At times," she said:

> I feel like a dry, dusty field that has been drenched
> by a fresh, spring rain, so sure am I of God's love for
> me. At other times I sense only blistering, cloudless
> days looming over the horizon. Dry spells deplete my
> strength once again, but I know I am not alone. I offer
> God my good intentions. I do my spiritual exercises.
> These fluctuations of light and shadow do not surprise
> or paralyze me anymore. I accept consolation and des-
> olation, certitude and uncertainty, as messengers of
> the divine, proclaiming the guidance I need at this mo-
> ment of my life.

My friend learned from personal experience that divine guidance
is a gift of transforming love. God led her step-by-step to where
he wanted her to go: into the promised land of likeness to his holy
will. As we travel on, and usually when we least expect it, "the dawn
from on high will break upon us" (Lk 1:78), and we shall be more
ready than ever to follow the Lord toward a new day.

The saints inspire us to put on the mind of Christ and to
live in humble gratitude to our dearest companion. When the
moment to witness to Christ is upon us, we stand shoulder to
shoulder with these holy defenders of the Faith, who never sepa-
rated credal truths from their implementation in daily life. With
them, we pray:

You order all things graciously.
You are the mystery
unfolding cosmos and humanity.
You are my homeland,
my most original ground.
Your Presence
welds all things together.
You are the caring love
that carries me
like mother earth
does forest, flower, tree.
Outside you
the world is a wilderness,
the universe indifferent,
the earth a barren planet,
and I a speck of dust.
Your Presence alone
is lasting home;
you are the Beyond
in the midst of daily life,
the sacrament of everydayness:
immersion in daily duty
as flowing from your hand
is homecoming to you.

Pause and Ponder

- Have I begun to see the narrow way as the one and
  only road that leads to the fullness of everlasting
  life?
- What helps me to overcome the temptation to detour from the path I ought to follow, especially
  when I feel discouraged by its rigor?

Becoming an Instrument of Justice, Peace, and Mercy

Avoiding Singularity and Offering Care in Christ's Name

I run the way of your commandments,
for you enlarge my understanding.

Psalm 119:32

On the narrow way, we shed the adolescent baggage of becoming a self-sufficient personality. We avoid singularity and self-posturing and adopt the sober commitment characteristic of an adult life of Christian love. Saint Benedict recommended in this regard that the monks avoid attending to their own plans and projects over and above the common rules governing the monastery. Good superiors, he noted, work for the common good. They do not seek special treatment but relish the richness of the ordinary. In this way, they become more just, more at peace with themselves, and more merciful toward others. We do the same when we proclaim in the course of fulfilling our call the beauty and benefits that are ours and when we do what God asks of us with a song in our heart and a smile on our lips.

Saint Ita, whose name means "thirst for holiness," was a sixth-century virgin, from royal Irish stock, who founded a monastery and ran a school for boys. Many future saints of Ireland came under her care, including Saint Brendan (484–577). One day he asked his teacher if she could tell him the three things most pleasing to God. She replied without hesitation: "true faith with a pure heart; a simple life with a grateful spirit; and generosity inspired by charity." He then asked her what three things most displeased God. Her answer: a mouth that hates people; a heart harboring resentments; and confidence in wealth. Though Saint Ita's monastery has been in ruins since the ninth century, pilgrims still place flowers among the stones at her burial site, praying to know the love of God that enables them to cultivate Christ's presence day after day.

The lesson this saint teaches is that when we offer care in Christ's name, our ministry of justice, peace, and mercy can remain pliable enough to meet the needs at hand and patient enough to address any demand that arises. It becomes second nature to us to understand what others really feel; to confirm their value in God's eyes; and to illumine their sense of life's purpose. Knowing that their condition is as wounded as ours, we do what we can to show them how much we really care.

The love of the Lord flows forth in physical healings (the blind see) and spiritual transformations (the adulteress sins no more). We become conveyors of this love in such healing professions as those of social workers, nurses, and first responders, and in the therapy provided by counselors and spiritual directors. Whatever service we offer in Christ's name, we do so with self-giving love. It becomes second nature to us to aid those who suffer from abandonment of body and soul. As we follow the narrow way, we try to be sensitive and responsive healers, bringing the light of Christ to the lonely, the sad, the disheartened. We avoid the pitfalls associated with exalted ministerial projects or self-congratulatory heroics, preferring to live the paradox of "having nothing, and yet possessing everything" (2 Cor 6:10).

Balancing Sensitivity and Responsibility

To maintain this balance, we must never view others as interruptions. Whenever someone comes to us, even if we are in the middle of another task, we must recognize that they are inviting us to see Jesus in them. This way of seeing makes us sensitive to their feelings while we seek responsible ways to foster a more just, peaceful, and merciful world.

Our commitment to become the eyes, the hands, the feet of Jesus — his instruments for good on this planet — initiates the right rhythm of sensitivity and responsibility. We pause long enough to consider what others are feeling so that our response will be the best one for them.

As we strive to deflect attention from ourselves and show care in Christ's name and fulfill our call, we must cultivate certain dispositions, beginning with social reverence. St. Teresa of Calcutta consoled the poor, sick, and dying in the streets of her teeming city with tender care. She did not ask them about their faith, their background, their moral standards, or their education. She treated each of them with the love of the Divine Mystery in whom she believed with her whole heart. For her, each wretched body she bathed and fed was like a venerable shrine because there Christ himself appeared. Following the saint's example, we also must allow reverence to suffuse our communal commitments and grant our service both depth and radiance. This first disposition enables us to honor the hidden nobility of every person.

A second disposition to cultivate is personal respect. It cautions us to pay detailed attention to the dignity of life while opposing every form of social injustice that keeps us from showing compassion for our own and others' vulnerability. Personal respect keeps us from becoming oblivious to the plight of the spiritually abandoned.

A third disposition is that of appealing to what is noblest in others. Calling forth the gifts and talents of others helps them, as it does us, to find and fulfill their calling in Christ. It also combats any unjust, merciless repudiation of others' giftedness, instead inviting them to consider the challenges and changes the Lord asks of them on their way to heaven.

Being in Harmony with Christ

To appreciate what it means to offer care in Christ's name, we must grow beyond the subtle traps of self-gratification and ruthless acquisition. These obliterate the Golden Rule of doing unto others what we pray they will do unto us.

Harmony with Christ helps us to resist the impulse to escape what is unpleasant or to refuse to see the grain of truth in every criticism. It encourages us, no matter how busy we are, to lay aside our schedules when someone needs us; to suspend our fear of failure when life demands that we step out of our comfort zone; and to live up to our promise of fidelity in service of the Gospel directive to "make disciples of all nations" (Mt 28:19).

The opposite of harmony with Christ is the hypocrisy he abhorred: "This people honors me with their lips, but their hearts are far from me; in vain do they worship me, teaching human precepts as doctrines" (Mt 15:8–9). Difficult as it may be, we must avail ourselves of the grace to appreciate what is precious in others. In doing so, we grow beyond the rampant individualism that destroys our spiritual communion in Christ and that sows seeds of discord in our faith community.

Caring in Christ's Name

Chaplains, retreat masters, social workers, doctors, nurses, pastors, spiritual counselors, ministers, psychotherapists, teachers, spouses, parents, soul-friends — all these people are caregivers, who know what it means to go outside of themselves; to forget their own needs; and to focus on the cry of the materially poor and spiritually abandoned.

The primary condition that makes caregiving effective is humility. No one is superhuman. Everyone, even the most skilled and energetic among us, has physical, emotional, and spiritual limits to submit to the healing touch of the Lord.

A second condition for walking the narrow way is detachment from the illusion that we can address problems without recourse to divine grace. To reach inside our sinful heart and find a ray of hope, we must cease to rely on our own cleverness and place ourselves and others under the canopy of God's care.

The third and most important condition for effective caregiving is that we try to express unconditional love for others as children of God. What matters is to reconfirm our commitment to Christ to feed his lambs and tend his sheep (see Jn 21:15–17), not only when we feel like it but whenever he asks, not because of what they can do for us, but because of what God asks us to do for them. When we do this, we find as we minister to them that they in fact minister to us.

Unlike impersonal service, caregiving inspired by Christ addresses the inmost needs of persons in every social setting. Each activity we perform bears the imprint of our willingness to follow generations of walkers, who find their strength, as the prophet Isaiah says, "in quietness and in trust" (Is 30:15).

It is difficult to be still and wait upon the Lord in a cultural climate where instant gratification is preferable to shepherding the sacred dimension of reality. A "get it over and done with now" mentality tempts us to live as if we were in the emergency room of a hospital. From what does waiting save us? From acting without sufficient reflection. From thoughtless consumption in a throw-away culture. From sharp-tongued barbs that hurt others' feelings. Instead, waiting allows us to give God time to show us the way we ought to follow.

Waiting *upon* the word of the Lord is different from waiting *for* this or that event to happen. Addressing those in need of our care soothes their fears and strengthens us for what lies ahead. These virtues save us from clock-bound pressures; they draw us into the peaceful ebb and flow of being with the Lord and doing what he commands.

Stillness is a divine gift that enables us to hear the whispers of the Holy Spirit in minds often inundated by the clamor of endless noise. We silence our own ideas and listen to the still, small voice of God. Such listening allows us to grow in the cardinal virtues of prudence, justice, fortitude, and temperance. Prudence invites us to consider the spiritual depth or shallowness of our perhaps up to now unexamined life. Justice reminds us to respect our own and others' dignity and the right to life that marks us as the people of God. Fortitude guarantees that our commitment to offer care in Christ's name will never waver. Temperance readies us for whatever sacrifices fulfilling our call exacts of us.

Our answer to God's call silences debates and defenses and becomes an expression of confidence in the Word made flesh who dwells among us. When we are at our weakest, Christ manifests himself as our strength. When we wonder if assistance is at hand, we simply reply, "Our help is in the name of the LORD, / who made heaven and earth" (Ps 124:8). Our happiness lies not in instant gratification but in nurturing our passion for the impossible under the sovereignty of our Savior. Faith in his word reveals the falsehood embedded in pessimistic acceptance of a predetermined fate. We grow in likeness to Christ not on the basis of our own cleverness but because of a profound, inner change of heart.

That kind of change does not come about by our own strength of will or intelligence, but only through the grace of God. So generous is this gift that, however many times we detour away from God, God never deserts us. While we may not know the day or the hour set for the coming of the Lord, nothing can shake our certitude that he will shatter our deafness and speak a word of comfort to our souls.

A sure sign that the Lord reigns over our lives is our being ready and willing to offer care in his name. The evangelist John expresses this new commandment in words worthy of being etched on our hearts: "We know love by this, that he laid down his life for us — and we ought to lay down our lives for one another. How does God's love abide in anyone who has the world's goods and sees a brother or sister in need and yet refuses to help?" (1 Jn 3:16–17). To uphold the rights of others in justice, to be peacemakers at home and throughout the world, to feed, shelter, and clothe the least of these in acts of mercy and charity are among the many ways we offer care in Christ's name. That care is the common bond that characterizes a Christian community, and so we pray:

> Like a stained-glass window filters
> the radiance of the sun in countless colors,
> make us light up the corner of the universe
> where we are placed in time and space

like candles in a dark and empty hall,
laying down our life little by little
in service of all who pass our way in history.
Let our love be strong and honest,
never a refuge from reality and suffering,
not sentimental, but impeccably right and fair,
so that not we, but you may rise in the heart
of the multitudes in search of
a shepherd for their lives.

Pause and Ponder

- Becoming an instrument of justice, peace, and mercy involves a daily *yes* to God. Have I begun to make this affirmation both an essential part of my life of prayer and the foundation of my care for others?
- What expressions of self-giving love have I practiced today and how have others benefited from them?

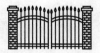

Part Three

Enter Through the Narrow Gate

For this reason I bow my knees before the Father, from whom every family in heaven and on earth takes its name. I pray that, according to the riches of his glory, he may grant that you may be strengthened in your inner being with power through his Spirit, and that Christ may dwell in your hearts through faith, as you are being rooted and grounded in love. I pray that you may have the power to comprehend, with all the saints, what is the breadth and length and height and depth, and to know the love of Christ that surpasses knowledge, so that you may be filled with all the fullness of God. Now to him who by the power at work within us is able to accomplish abundantly far more than all we can ask or imagine, to him be glory in the church and in Christ Jesus to all generations, forever and ever. Amen.

Ephesians 3:14–21

STEP NINE
Keep Custody Over Our Tongue and Listen More Than We Speak

Renewing Our Mission and Ministry in Christ

Lead me in the path of your commandments,
for I delight in it.

Psalm 119:35

In the ninth degree of humility, Benedict counsels us to restrain our garrulous tongues (talking, texting, tweeting, in our day) and to value the silence that leads us to speak the truth.

Failure to control our tongue and listen more than we speak can deplete our energy physically, emotionally, and spiritually. In the words of the apostle James, "no one can tame the tongue — a restless evil, full of deadly poison. With it we bless the Lord and Father, and with it we curse those who are made in the likeness of God. From the same mouth come blessing and cursing" (Jas 3:8–10). Seeing how grumbling, murmuring, and gossiping exhaust us, is it any wonder that even our best efforts produce few worthwhile results?

Though this lack of self-control may repeat itself more than we like to admit, each time it does we can see it as a positive challenge to strengthen our dedication and renew our desire to avoid the emptiness of idle chatter. We collect our thoughts before engaging in bellicose arguments to score points over our opponents. Many texts from Holy Scripture inspire the counsel not to speak until someone asks us to do so or until we have to answer pertinent questions. Why is this love for silence so strong in the Benedictine rule, and why ought we to try to restore more silence in our personal and communal lives? In Proverbs 10:19 we read: "When words are many, transgression is not lacking." And in Proverbs 18:21 we hear this stark warning: "Death and life are in the power of the tongue." We all remember the reminder we may have received from parents and teachers that if we cannot find something good to say about a person, then it is better to say nothing at all.

On this step along the narrow way, empty chatter attracts us less and less. We prefer moments of silence to noisy fillers. We long to obey Psalm 46:10, "Be still, and know that I am God!" We pray that the words we use will ring with truth and be edifying to others.

Benedict believes that silence is a sanctuary in which we experience intimacy with God. It produces a heightened capacity for meditation, prayer, and contemplation. In that silent center of wordless adoration, we can often hear the Holy Spirit praying in our hearts. As still as a child on its mother's lap (see Ps

131), we are with God and God is with us. We are wordlessly present to one another, yet a world of communication transpires between us.

This deep silence is not meant to produce spiritual highs. Saint Benedict always returns us to the richness of the ordinary. It simply warms our heart, revealing to us in the midst of the ups and downs of daily life that we stand on the firm ground of God's unchanging love. We listen more than we speak and renew the depth dimension of our mission and ministry in Christ.

Listening to the Guidance of God

Our dependence on the guidance of God is not a sign of weakness; it is our greatest gift.

Grace lifts us beyond our fear of missing the mark, beyond our lack of vision and our proneness to deception; it enables us to surrender to the "how much more" of God's love for us: "But the free gift is not like the trespass. For if the many died through the one man's trespass, much more surely have the grace of God and the free gift in the grace of the one man, Jesus Christ, abounded for the many" (Rom 5:15).

Scripture assures us that before we come into existence, God already knows our essence, our true calling, in his mind and heart. He says in the words of the prophet, "I have called you by name, you are mine" (Is 43:1).

Divine guidance is beyond what any temporal phase of life can convey. It is like the rush of a mighty ocean streaming through every millisecond of our pilgrimage on earth. The more we see our numbered days with the eyes of faith, the less we are in danger of succumbing to false or confusing directives to follow.

Even if nothing seems to be happening, humanly speaking, much is transpiring, divinely speaking. In due time we will see, as in a tapestry, the threads that weave together the God-guided moments of our past, present, and future life. This intricate weaving encompasses each and every disclosure of what Christ was, is, and will be on the narrow way to heaven's door.

God may grace us at times with a unique epiphany of his presence. If we remember that our lives are a gradually unfolding tapestry, we will not exalt such a spiritual experience out of context. We will see it as episodic, as a prism reflecting flashes of God's overall guidance in our own and others' lives.

The deeper we dive into the ocean of God's loving presence, the more we learn to rely on the graces prepared for us from the beginning. Grace is there to help us cope with cloudy days and stormy nights. There is no need to fear even in the darkest storm or on the roughest sea.

Grace is indispensable for us to abandon the illusion of independent, do-it-yourself direction and to accept our dependence on the guidance of God. Only through the miracle of grace can we walk the narrow way and discover where we were meant by God to go.

This mysterious guidance, this unsurpassed gift, transforms our lost and lonely lives into a "new creation" (2 Cor 5:17). We are radiant with the wisdom of the Incarnate Lord through whom we experience, in the course of trying to fulfill our call, that we are searchers, pilgrims, sojourners — always striving, never arriving. At times we travel fearfully, at other times faithfully, toward our goal of union with God.

Despite momentary uncertainty, our Divine Caller continues to communicate himself to us. When we do become aware of the depth dimension of our mission and ministry, we are free to accept or refuse that to which we are being led. God does not force a response. Neither can we predict the way the Spirit would have us go, nor the kind of guidance we will receive. What happens in this realm remains a mystery known fully only to the Trinity. Our task is to trust. Even when we come to know our call, its implications will still exceed our grasp; but, having traveled this far, we have no intention of retracing our steps.

Everyday events, seen from the perspective of faith, become signposts on the road that leads to abundant life. A chance meeting between strangers on a plane becomes more revealing than we could have predicted. A discriminatory situation in our community challenges us to practice compassion. A beggar at our door appeals to our charity and prompts us to reexamine if we really see our Lord in the least of these.

From the moment we awaken in the morning to when we retire at night, we try to listen to all that transpires as a reminder of God's loving attention to the details of our daily life. If he cares for sparrows and counts the hairs on our head (see Lk 12:6–7), how can we doubt that he cares for us?

Renewing Our Mission and Ministry in Christ

The fruits of silence, reading, meditation, prayer, and contemplation are at work in our personal lives and in the entire Church. These spiritual exercises form an essential part of our ministry. We want to deepen our inner resources so that we can become more faithful instruments of God in family life, Church, and society. We know that holiness is not a private possession granted to select souls but a universal call issued to each of us. It is not identical with ecstatic feelings or extraordinary phenomena. Holiness is loving God with our whole being and radiating that love in every dimension of our life and world.

Flowing from contemplation and all that readies us for this gift is the life of dedicated, Christlike service. If service does not have sufficient roots in contemplative presence, it may lead to arrogance and activism out of touch with our pursuit of the narrow way. We work to attain our own success with little consideration for what God may be asking of us.

In stillness, we can listen to God's directives and do our best to execute them gently but firmly in the given situation. Whether we succeed or fail is not the point. What counts for God is our willingness to try. Contemplation enables us to be serenely present in the world, doing what we can, without succumbing to the ways of the world. We maintain roots in the love of God while going forth in labors for the kingdom.

This rhythm of recollection and participation is an essential feature of Christian commitment. Whatever we happen to be doing — cooking a meal, writing a letter, teaching a class, nursing the sick — we do out of love for God and a desire to make this love manifest. We want to help others see God's face in every person, event, and thing. This is what it means as Christians to be on mission. Missionary duty is not limited to evangelizing work in foreign lands. It is what we are to do every day in our homes and professions. Whatever our position or profession, we have to remain faithful disciples.

There is no split between who we are and what we do. We display outwardly the spiritual values we treasure inwardly. Others sense this caring presence when they say, "Your heart is really in your work, isn't it?" That is why they may remember, "It was not so much what you said or did so well but the way you were. That meant more to me than words can express, and I'll always be grateful."

To believe in the ultimate goodness of life, to hope that things will be better tomorrow than they are today, to love those entrusted to our care — these three virtues correct the problems of discouragement, depletion of dedication, and closure to compassion. We can be gentle and kind because we recognize how vulnerable all of us are. We can live in peace despite the tension that will always be present in every human situation.

If we are at peace within ourselves, not demanding perfection, then we can be peacemakers for others. We can never underestimate the power of being *a living witness* to what we believe. In this regard, actions do speak louder than words. People remember who we are, even if they do not recall exactly what we said or did.

To become givers as well as receivers of care, we must purify our love of self-gratifying passions. Others are not the objects of our pleasure but precious people we ought to treat with compassion, be they young or old, healthy or infirm.

A fellow parishioner extends a sign of Christ's peace, and we acknowledge it warmly. A woman lowers the window on the driver's side of her car and asks us for directions; we pull over and take the time to draw her a map. A passenger next to us on a plane asks if we will change seats with him because the window side makes him nervous, and we oblige with a smile. Encounters like these, however nondescript, are life-giving. They exemplify respect for our mutual, God-given dignity. As members of Christ's Mystical Body, as participants in the life of the Trinity, we try our best to minister in a kind and caring way to others through Christ.

Such loving care heals the fractured relations that result when vice prevails over virtue, when division replaces respect for diversity, when indifference triumphs over addressing neighborly needs.

A frequent temptation we face is spiritual laziness, accompanied by the temptation to complacency. Both vices make it impossible for us to listen to the invitations, challenges, and appeals sent to us by the Holy Spirit, who seeks to remind us that "we are God's co-workers … God's field, God's building" (1 Cor 3:9, NABRE).

On our walk, we have to go through dry and rainy seasons, but at every step on the way God cultivates the seeds of faith planted in the field of our heart. "If you have faith the size of a mustard seed … nothing will be impossible for you" (Mt 17:20). Setbacks and afflictions are not endpoints but openings to increase our belief that "God is faithful, and he will not let [us] be tested beyond [our] strength" (1 Cor 10:13). God knows that all of us have bodily, mental, and spiritual fractures and wounds due to sin. We beg for healing, and God repeats, "Fear not, I am with you always" (see Mt 28:20).

Being in Communion with the Lord

Despite our desire to be in communion with the Lord, our arrogant, isolated "I" sometimes prevails over the needs of those God calls us to serve. When this happens we become "ministerial functionaries," trying to force the situations in which we find ourselves to conform to our plans and projects. This kills empathy; it triggers the need for compulsive control. We find rationalizations to explain away the inability to restrain our tongue. This compulsion to be in control prevents the emergence of our full personhood in Christ. It blocks the forgiveness our Redeemer grants to us.

In cooperation with the grace of God, we let go of anxious feelings and flights of fantasy. We begin to understand that the way to renew our mission and ministry is not to seek refuge in the shelter of irrational imaginings, but to build bridges between suffering and striving humanity, and not to leave anyone behind. We long to experience, with God's help, greater dedication to duty, increased honesty in human relations, and better contributions to the upbuilding of the world.

These values cannot be forced. They emerge when we rise above self-centered deeds and decisions and listen more than we speak. Seldom does God use a bullhorn to attract our attention. God prefers gentle breezes to thunderclaps, quiet whispers to loud clamors. To receive divine blessings, we may have to leave behind us crowded corridors and noisy rooms and seek in solitude the sounds of silence that whisper, "God is near."

We rejoice, not in our own ability to overcome faults, but in

God's promise to show us the way home. We make it a habit to abide with simple signs of the mystery: a dewdrop on a blade of grass, a humming insect pollinating a flower, a budding rose, a baby robin testing its wings. We hear the cadence of nature and the music of the spheres. We appreciate anew sights and sounds familiar to us: the howling of the wind, the pitter-patter of the rain, the footsteps of a passerby, the whimpering of a child, the whirring of workmen's tools.

Such experiences do not require excessive wit or stores of information. We listen more than we speak. We bridle our tongue, and we talk together about what matters most to us. We create a climate that results in the sharing of wisdom, while admitting that in and of ourselves we have no strength at all. We are powerless unless we dare to confess that it is the Lord who empowers us, and so we pray:

> Thank you, Lord,
> for your walking on this earth
> as one of us.
> You were a living message
> of forming love.
> May your love be the center
> around which our life forms itself
> like a shell around an oyster
> with its priceless pearl.
> Melt all resistance
> when your love begins to fashion
> our heart and its feelings.
> Make us sense
> the silent stream of love
> that flows into humanity
> from the mystery of the Trinity.

Pause and Ponder

- When uncertainty strikes, do I take the time to pray, asking for divine guidance and never succumbing to the illusion that I can walk this way alone?
- When I slip onto a path of perdition, do I immediately seek forgiveness? Do I look for counsels on how not to deviate from the narrow way and try my best to listen to them?

STEP TEN
Cultivating Christ's Presence Day by Day

Revitalizing Our Faith Community

When I told of my ways, you answered me;
teach me your statutes.

Psalm 119:26

There was a road between Jerusalem and the village of Emmaus, a distance, Scripture tells us, of about seven miles (see Lk 24:13–35). It was most likely a narrow way, a walking path roughly paved and certainly not a smooth highway. On it walked two seekers, who talked about what had transpired over the past few days.

As they pondered these mysterious events, a stranger joined them. He asked what they were discussing so intently. They told him about a prophet, Jesus of Nazareth, who had been handed over to the chief priests, condemned to death, and crucified. They had lost their hopes of victory. They would have liked to see him do what a great worldly king would have done — redeem Israel with a show of mighty power.

The stranger listened. They told him how early that very morning, some women had gone to the tomb and did not find Jesus' body. Instead, they saw angels who said he was alive. Wonder collided with disbelief, but the stranger did not flinch. Knowing they would soon reach the wrong outcome, he interpreted the Scriptures for them. The life of the Messiah would not end in a display of worldly power, which leads to perdition, but in the powerlessness of the cross. That is where true victory is to be found.

What began as a narrowing of their hopes ended in the saving narration of a world redeemed. Wanting to know about the truth of God's word, they asked him to stay with them when they reached their destination. Walking and talking with him on the road had left a burning sensation in their hearts. At table, Jesus blessed and broke the bread and, in the company of this newly formed faith community, he revealed who he was. No sooner did they see that he was the risen Lord than he vanished.

Immediately, they returned to Jerusalem and found the Eleven with "their companions gathered together" (Lk 24:33). What had happened to them on the road to Emmaus would be a testimony to the Resurrection. Thereafter, Jesus would reveal himself to them in the breaking of the bread. They who are many would be "one body, for we all partake of the one bread" (1 Cor 10:17).

The formation of a Christian community around the Eucharistic table is a mystery unfolding age upon age. Such a transformed community is inexplicable in terms of human power or persuasion because "the cup of blessing that we bless, is it not a sharing in the blood of Christ? The bread that we break, is it not a sharing in the body of Christ?" (1 Cor 10:16).

Revitalizing Christian community is the Spirit-inspired capacity to go beyond personality differences, anxious doubts, and ingrained prejudices. We benefit from the tenth step on Saint Benedict's ladder of humility by practicing prudence, by withholding quick-tempered mockery of others' ideas, and by avoiding derisive laughter and back-stabbing snickering.

The deepest affinity of Christian souls does not reside in a kindred collection of tastes, fashions, and styles of life, but in a bonding that comes from cultivating Christ's presence day by day. Together we pray that the Holy Spirit will help us to contribute to the common good and to celebrate our gifts, no matter how humble and hidden they may be: "speaking the truth in love, we must grow in every way into him who is the head, into Christ, from whom the whole body, joined and knit together by every ligament with which it is equipped, as each part is working properly, promotes the body's growth in building itself up in love" (Eph 4:15–16).

Fruits of Living in a Revitalized Faith Community

In the New Testament, the evangelists name many women, among them Anna, a prophetess (see Lk 2:36–38); Elizabeth, the mother of John the Baptist (Lk 1:5–58); Mary and Martha (Lk 10:38–42, Jn 11:1–37, and Jn 12:1–8); and Mary Magdalene, who helped to support Jesus' ministry (Lk 8:1–3), who stood at the foot of the cross (Mt 27:56), and who was the first to see Jesus after the Resurrection (Lk 24:1–12). Other women are named in the letters of Paul the apostle, including Phoebe (Rom 16:1) and Priscilla (or Prisca — Rom 16:3).

In Luke 8:1–3, we learn the names of the Galilean women who followed Jesus, including Mary Magdalene, Joanna, and Susanna. Though we do not know their names, we do know that Jesus healed Peter's mother-in-law (see Mt 8:14–15) and the daughter of Jarius (Mk 5:22–43). Similarly, there are five notable episodes during which Jesus encounters unnamed women whose lives he changes forever and who become true heroines of Christian history.

The first of the unnamed women whose faith is like a force of nature is one suffering from a hemorrhage (see Lk 8:43–48). She was among the poor souls in the crowd following Jesus and pressing in upon him. At the risk of being trampled, she propelled herself forward. For twelve years she had suffered from this affliction and spent all her money on physicians, none of whom cured her. This was her last chance. She was unable to see Jesus face to face. Her only option was to come from behind him and do something so small, so unassuming, that faith alone emboldened her. She stretched out her hand and touched the fringe of his cloak. She may have closed her eyes and prayed in sheer desperation for him to help her when, lo and behold, her hemorrhage stopped. Jesus stopped, too, and asked who touched him. No one had an answer. Given the size of the crowd raging like an out-of-control river around him, how could anyone know who touched him? Yet Jesus felt a flood of healing power being released from him. He knew some contact had been made. It was impossible for the woman to stay hidden. She came forward. The crowds probably cleared a path so she could approach him in fear and trembling. She was the one who touched him, the one he healed. Jesus relieved her anxiety and said that her faith had made her well and that she could go forth in peace.

We identify with this heroine of faith; we applaud what she did. When we suffer from bodily and spiritual sickness, when we feel unworthy to so much as touch the hem of his garment, we rely on Jesus to save us. We are this woman, pressing beyond any illusion of self-salvation and seeking to know Jesus by means of the naked depth of our faith. We want to emulate her boldness and appeal directly to the healing heart of Jesus. She becomes for us a model of how to call upon the Lord to release his power and rescue us.

This encounter proves that Jesus treated women, often in defiance of cultural norms, with respect. They could trust him because he transcended patriarchal systems and met his followers, male and female, in respect for their dignity. They broke protocol to follow him, and he rewarded them with the grace of redemption. Perhaps now that Jesus had cured her, this unnamed woman sought and was granted admission to full discipleship. The power of Jesus that empowered her made her living proof of his saving mission in the world.

This same virtue of holy boldness characterizes the Syrophoenician woman's faith (see Mk 7:24–30). Jesus had gone to this region, thinking he could rest a while in a nondescript house that would accommodate him. There he could be alone in silence and solitude. It was not to be. A woman whose little daughter was the target of an unclean spirit heard that he was there and rushed to find him, for many already knew of his power to dispel demons. Though she was a Gentile woman, she begged Jesus to banish the demon from her beloved daughter. The conversation they exchanged opened the door to Jesus' mission of salvation to all people.

To test her, Jesus said matter-of-factly that the Jewish people had first rights to his food, his word, and that it was not fair to take it from them and throw it "to the dogs," for that is what the Jewish people thought of Gentiles. The woman's answer moved Jesus' heart. She replied that even dogs crouching under the table get to eat the children's crumbs. So startling was her statement of faith that Jesus not only complimented her for saying it; he also saved her daughter. She could go home to the wondrous news that the demon had left the little girl. When the woman arrived there, her child was lying in bed, freed from any sign of demonic disruption. The mother's intercession had saved her child and forecasted the mission of Jesus to the Gentiles.

Like the first woman who suffered from painful bleeding, so, too, this Syrophoenician woman knew there was no one else to turn to but Jesus. In desperation, she sought his help. One woman touched his garment; the other prostrated herself at his feet. In both cases, their faith gained precedence over any forethought. They acted spontaneously, seeking from Jesus the healing and freeing touch they most needed. His power went out to them, in one incidence to stop a hemorrhage, in the other to cast out a demon.

Because these women believed in him, they did not let anything dissuade them from following him on the narrow way; they acted on pure faith and were changed forever by the force of Jesus' physical and spiritual healing.

The third woman offers us a stunning example of just how "countercultural" Jesus was. When her healing occurred, he was teaching in one of the synagogues on the Sabbath (see Lk 13:10–17). Almost out of nowhere, there appeared a woman struggling with a spirit that had crippled her for eighteen years. Everyone must have stared at her. She was bent over and unable to stand up straight. Jesus beheld the true person that she was. He called her to come near, saying, "Woman, you are set free from your ailment" (Lk 13:12). He laid his hands upon her and she stood tall, amid what must have been astonishment on the part of the assembly. Her first thought was to praise God. The leader of the synagogue, on the other hand, berated Jesus for daring to cure anyone on the Sabbath. In no uncertain terms, he reminded the crowd that work could be done on six days but not on the seventh.

Jesus broke protocol and denounced his critics as hypocrites! Did they not untie their ox or donkey on the Sabbath to give it water? How could he refuse to loosen the bonds that had tied this woman in knots for eighteen years? Was she not a daughter of Abraham? Did she not deserve to be free on the Sabbath of all days? Thanks to her brave appearance and Jesus' intervention on her behalf, she was made whole in body and soul. What occurred put his opponents to shame. Instead of castigating him, the entire crowd felt embarrassed. Then they began to rejoice because of "all the wonderful things he was doing" (Lk 13:17).

The story of Jesus' encounter with the Samaritan woman in John 4:1–42 offers us a glimpse of the Master's gift of spiritual direction and its life-altering consequences. At the start of this encounter with the fourth unnamed woman, we learn that Jesus was tired out by his journey and, around noon, sat down by Jacob's well near the Samaritan city of Sychar. A Samaritan woman came there to draw water. Upon seeing her, Jesus asked her to give him a drink. This request startled her. Jesus' Jewish identity took her aback, since she was a woman of Samaria. After all, everyone knew that Jews do not share anything with Samaritans, let alone a common cup. Then Jesus made the surprising claim that he not only needed water to quench his thirst, but that he would also give her in return "living water." She did not know what he meant. What she did see was that he himself had no bucket. The well was deep. So from whence would he get this living water? Jacob and his sons and his flock had to drink from this well, so what could this kind of water be?

Jesus replied with a common-sense observation. Anyone who drinks water from a well will be thirsty again, but whoever drinks "living water" — the water he had come to give — would never be thirsty. The water of which he spoke would be "a spring of water gushing up to eternal life" (Jn 4:14).

The woman clung to his every word. She wanted this water so she would never again be thirsty and never have to come to the well again to fill her bucket. Central to her was her own comfort. Now it was time for Jesus to break through her literal interpretations and begin to appeal to her heart. He told her to go and call her husband and then return to the well. She answered that she had no husband. Jesus confirmed this truth. Then he declared to her astonishment that she had had five husbands and was now living with someone out of wedlock.

Instantly their encounter shifted from casual inquiry to pure wonder. She knew that she was talking to no ordinary Jew, but to a prophet. Her people worshipped on this mountain, whereas the Jewish people worshipped in Jerusalem. Once again, she highlighted how different they were, but Jesus would have none of it. Then, in response to her obvious eagerness to learn more, he offered a true prophecy, saying, "Woman, believe me, the hour is coming when you will worship the Father neither on this mountain nor in Jerusalem ... the hour is coming, and is now here, when the true worshippers will worship the Father in spirit and truth ... God is spirit, and those who worship him must worship in spirit and truth" (Jn 4:21–24).

From this point on, their exchange becomes increasingly revelatory. The woman says that the Messiah, who is called Christ, is coming, and that when he comes he will proclaim everything to us. Then Jesus shares with this woman, sinner though she is, one of his most revealing "I am" statements: "I am he, the one who is speaking to you" (Jn 4:26).

At that moment his disciples returned; they showed astonishment to find him speaking to the likes of her, but they said nothing. They only saw how the woman left her water jar by the well and ran back to the city, announcing to anyone with ears to hear to come and see the man who told her all that she had ever done, the man who just might be the Messiah! Many others came to believe because of her testimony. He accepted their invitation to stay with them for two days by which time they, too, had come to believe — not because of what she said, but because of what they had seen — that he truly was the Savior of the world.

The fifth unnamed woman bore the dreadful label of adulteress, a crime that deserved at that time the punishment of death by stoning. The scene between her and Jesus took place early in the morning at the Temple where he was teaching (see Jn 8:1–11). Bent on trying to trap him, the scribes and pharisees brought before him a woman guilty of adultery — caught in the very act — who, according to Mosaic law, had to be put to death. What did Jesus have to say about that? Clearly, they were testing him, but he did not engage in vain reasoning that might have led to their bringing some charges against him. Instead he bent down and wrote something on the ground with his finger. They continued to badger him with questions, but he kept on writing. What? Perhaps a list of their sins. They had to have been able to read what he wrote. The more they questioned him, the more he wrote, until finally he stood up and said, "Let anyone among you who is without sin be the first to throw a stone at her" (Jn 8:7). Again he bent down and continued to write on the ground. And one by one they retreated from the scene, starting with the elders.

Jesus was left alone with the woman. He glanced around and asked her where her accusers were. Has no one condemned her? No, she answered, not one. And, said Jesus, "Neither do I." Then he offered her these few but unforgettable, life-changing words: "Go your way, and from now on do not sin again" (Jn 8:11).

These five women model the full range of what it means to walk with Jesus on the narrow way. He goes against the system that would have banished them to the scrap heap of history and proclaims in each instance their equality in dignity. He changes their lives forever, and in the process he changes ours. The encounters between Jesus and these women exemplify what it means to cultivate Christ's presence with gentleness, sensitivity, and discretion. These virtues are the keys to revitalizing our faith community and growing daily in discipleship.

We suffer. We intercede for those less fortunate than we. We long to be free from ailments of body, mind, and spirit. We need the grace of ongoing conversion. And we long for forgiveness of our sins.

These women had an encounter with Jesus that changed them forever. What he did for them, he does for us. All we have to do is follow his directive: "Ask, and it will be given to you; search, and you will find; knock, and the door will be opened for you" (Mt 7:7).

What binds us into one body as a Christian community is not a technique we master but a living expression of our timeless call to participate in the life of the Trinity. On the narrow way, we would never think of "lording it over" another since we strive for daily conformity to Christ and to connect what we learn with how we live. Days of recollection that renew us spiritually do not result in a flight from reality but in a better way to cope with family problems, loss of employment, debilitating illnesses, and the death of loved ones. We do what we can to evangelize those fallen away from the Faith and to become practitioners of ongoing formation.

Fruits of living in a revitalized faith community include:

- Dying to the illusion that our individual or our corporate ego is all-powerful and acknowledging our dependency on the grace of God for plans fulfilled and failures incurred;
- Praying not only at special moments but in the mundane events that comprise our everyday life in the world;
- Abandoning ourselves to God in the ordinary give-and-take of daily life as well as during special occasions of ritual and worship;
- Making of our heart an oratory where we can withdraw from time to time to converse with Jesus with as much fervor and intimacy as possible.

Experiencing Communion with Christ

To be in communion with Christ is to let his love flow through us to all who live under its benevolent light — from the carpenter who fixes our roof to the terminally ill person who begs for our prayers. Entering through the narrow gate leaves no room for narcissism or the prejudices that paralyze our bestowal of Christ's compassion on others. As a faith community, we must "go and learn what this means, 'I desire mercy, not sacrifice.' For I have come to call not the righteous but sinners" (Mt 9:13).

The more we allow communion with Christ to guide us, the more we acknowledge our desire not to miss any occasion to revitalize our faith community. Expressing such care requires taking a risk. What if we do not receive in kind what we give to others? Shall we grow hard of heart? Shall we sink into arrogance and activism out of touch with discipleship, or shall we excel in unshakable faith, enduring hope, and steadfast love for the Lord from everlasting to everlasting (see Ps 103:17–18)?

Whatever we do — cooking a meal, writing a letter, teaching a class, visiting the sick — we do out of love for God and a desire to make this love manifest. To see God's face in every person, event, and thing we encounter enables us to remain faithful disciples despite daily pressures.

Christ wants us to be members of a family where "there is no longer Jew or Greek ... slave or free ... male and female; for all of you are one in Christ Jesus" (Gal 3:28). This communion can only happen if we allow Jesus to teach us how to rise above human cruelty and the devastating indifference that hurts so many.

The light of God within us is meant to radiate through our personality into the situations in which we find ourselves. God transforms us by grace so that we can bring the fruits of this transformation to others. We are led on the narrow way to move from a fragmented to an integrated life centered in such virtues as trust, simplicity, patience, and generosity. Only if we live these virtues to the full can the seeds of cultivating Christ's presence bear lasting fruit.

Fostering the Narrow Way

Fr. Walter Ciszek, SJ (1904–1984), volunteered to study Russian in the hope of being a missionary to the Soviet Union. Instead he found himself on assignment in eastern Poland in 1938, where within a year he watched as Red Army troops invaded the country. Ciszek, with the confidence in God that has become his hallmark, saw the hand of Holy Providence in this event and joined the Polish refugees disguised as a worker.

Arriving in the labor camps of Russia, he intended to carry out his ministry in secret. Two years later, all hope of doing so faded when the Soviet secret police arrested him, and he disappeared, for all intents and purposes, without a trace. In fact, the police imprisoned him in solitary confinement in a notorious prison in Moscow, where his captors determined to wrest from him his confession as a spy.

Ciszek, whose cause for sainthood is now before the Church, tells of his struggle to keep the Faith, especially in his autobiographical book, *He Leadeth Me.* For him this horrifying prison became a school of prayer, a place where he had to find a way to discern the will of God in everyday circumstances, no matter how debilitating they were.

The key to his inner freedom and peace was his complete abandonment to God's always benevolent will, commingled with the refusal to give in to bitterness or despair. God's grace enabled him to move from the destructive prison of his enclosed ego to the peaceful arena provided by his vows of poverty, chastity, and obedience.

After serving his sentence of fifteen years of hard labor, he was released in 1963 and returned to his community in New York

City where he lived for the remaining twenty years of his life, serving as a spiritual guide and a saintly witness to his oft-stated conviction that "If God is for us, who can be against us?" He died at the age of eighty in the peace and joy of Jesus.

Like Father Walter, we too may hear others call us fools for trying to become a healing presence in this world. People may perceive us as a threat to the inhumane notion of survival of the fittest. Cultivating Christ's presence day by day is the foundation of revitalizing our faith community. Though people who appear to have chosen the road to perdition may mock us, that is no reason for us to lose hope.

We must continue to be Christ's witnesses despite opposition. He calls us to honor the infinite worth of each person as a member of the human family bound together in the Body of Christ. In days of rejoicing and nights of weeping, we remain with and for one another, turning our will over to God's will for us.

When life becomes burdensome, when feet that once ran swiftly on the narrow way become as heavy as lead, we ask the Lord to take our yoke upon his shoulders and strengthen our pace. We interweave our abiding with the Lord in contemplation with our willingness to act on behalf of others whom we learn to love without limit. We pray not so much for personal pleasure or contentment but for ways to extend the redemptive graces of the Lord to every believing and seeking soul, and so we pray:

Lord,
You entrusted this tiny planet
in your creation to us.
You set the timing
of conception in the womb,
of birth and of abiding,

of listening to every happening
as a sweet tiding
of your concelebration
of faith, hope, and love
in every community
blessed by your presence
in the breaking of the bread.

Pause and Ponder

- Do I have the fortitude to name those displays of worldly power that have led me to toy with paths of perdition rather than to rejoice in the powerlessness of the cross?
- What marks of conformity to Christ are most important in my life at the moment? And do I flinch when others call me foolish for following him?

STEP ELEVEN

Refusing to Murmur or Complain

Celebrating the Joy of Appreciative Living

Teach me, O LORD, the way of your statutes,
and I will observe it to the end.

Psalm 119:33

When we were infants, we had no choice but to be the center of our parents' attention. Selflessly pleasing them was out of the question. Sheer survival demanded that we cry when hungry or wet or uncomfortable. Our soggy diaper had to be changed at three in the morning. We could not stop howling and wait until mother and father awakened from sleep because for us the entire universe was wet, and someone had to dry it!

In infancy, because we were "his or her majesty, the baby," we could not yet fend for ourselves and so we had no choice but to whine and whimper. Our parents were givers; we were takers. Only as life went on did we progress from ego-centered to other-directed love that radiates affection for those who care for us.

Christ teaches us to love one another, not out of a sense of duty but because all of us are children of God. There are no strings attached to his love. During his earthly life, he healed lepers, the blind, the deaf, and those possessed by demons, and he did so because he cared personally for them. Any attempt on our part to express the depth of such love will always fall short of Christ's example, but still we must try our best to emulate it.

Though we ought to curb our tendency to murmur or complain, we do so anyway. Saint Benedict reminds us on the eleventh step of the ladder that we are to check ourselves before we veer in the direction of becoming joy-killers or mood-breakers. Good humor can lessen stress and tension and evoke joyful appreciation of one another. The opposite happens when we raise our voices in an effort to outshout one another. We lose the dignity of Christian comportment when we do not keep the promises we make to God and others. We hold onto hurts and withhold forgiveness. Sin increases, yet grace abounds (see Rom 5:20) every time compassion replaces condemnation and constructive options gain precedence over destructive actions.

We must avoid many pitfalls to enter the narrow gate and go forward with grace. No matter how dedicated and creative we try to be, we often experience less than satisfactory results. We want to celebrate the joy of appreciative living, and yet all too often this ideal fades away and never becomes a reality.

God cannot coerce a grateful response from us. The choice is ours: Do we believe so much in the benevolence of God that we can say thanks in good times and bad? Or do we find it impossible, amid the harshness of reality, to trust in the command to give thanks in all circumstances?

Giving with a grateful demeanor rests on the recognition that God provides us with "every blessing in abundance, so that by always having enough of everything, [we] may share abundantly in every good work" (2 Cor 9:8). We try never to murmur or complain because to do so violates the truth that every expression of thanks on our part produces "thanksgiving to God through us; for the rendering of this [virtue] not only supplies the needs of the saints but also overflows with many thanksgivings to God" (2 Cor 9:11–12).

To live appreciatively is to be generous, not greedy; courageous in our confession of the Gospel, not cowardly; pointing to the surpassing grace of God, not highlighting every failure and losing our faith.

Exercising the Power of Appreciation

The encounter between the deacon Philip and the Ethiopian eunuch, a court official of the queen, is one of the most touching accounts of the Sacrament of Baptism in the New Testament. This meeting with Philip did not have to happen, but it did (see Acts 8:26–39).

The eunuch had come to Jerusalem to worship and was on his way home, seated in his chariot. Of all things, he was reading the Prophet Isaiah. The Spirit said to Philip, "Go over to this chariot and join it" (Acts 8:29). Philip wasted no time doing what he was told. He ran over and heard the eunuch reading the words of the prophet and asked him if he understood them. He did not. He needed a guide to reveal their meaning. Philip got into the chariot and, like Jesus who interpreted the Scriptures to the two disciples on the road to Emmaus, Philip did the same. He connected the prophet's words about a sheep being led to the slaughter with the risen Lord. He proclaimed the good news about Jesus with such joy and conviction that the eunuch had only one request: to be baptized in a nearby stream. Then Scripture tells us: "When they came up out of the water, the Spirit of the Lord snatched Philip away; the eunuch saw him no more, and went on his way rejoicing" (Acts 8:39).

From this account we gather that entering the narrow way results in our recovery of the joy of appreciative living. Miracles like the eunuch's conversion, of the deacon being in the right place at the right time, do not have to happen, but they do. God blessed Philip's action and brought forth from it a celebration of conversion in which we all share. Christ changes "the body of our humiliation that it may be conformed to the body of his glory, by the power that also enables him to make all things subject to himself" (Phil 3:21).

We can only surmise that from that moment onward, the newly baptized eunuch radiated the unique image of Christ within him. His story helps us to believe this prophecy: "Let us not grow weary in doing what is right, for we will reap at harvest time, if we do not give up" (Gal 6:9). Jesus sends us the Paraclete to encourage us to let go of what we are not so that we can become other Christs, whose destiny is to love and serve the people of God.

The more we see ourselves as Christ's friends and followers, the more sure we are that the situation in which we find ourselves, the people we meet along the way, and the whole world are in God's hands. The power and practice of appreciation permeates all that we have done and will do now and in the future. Formative experiences like those associated with Eucharistic celebrations bolster our capacity for appreciation, just as deformative experiences like that of betrayal by a co-worker trigger depreciation. These experiences put us at another fork in the road. Which path will we choose: that which appreciates events as providential, however supportive or disappointing they may be? Or that which depreciates God's "so-called" guidance and severs us from humbly accepting what he sends us?

Appreciative abandonment to the mystery is a choice we have to make many times in our life. As we do so, we begin to detect in every happening a beneficial possibility that opens us to the depth of divine love. This disposition generates on our part a spontaneous grasp of the inspirations sent by the Holy Spirit. We become like Deacon Philip, attentive to any directives the mystery may disclose to us. There is no doubt that God will use the blessings we receive to benefit others.

This stance gives rise to the joyous assurance that even in the face of menacing and demeaning events, we can trust the Lord and try to see in every episode that tempts us to follow the path of perdition a call to deeper conversion.

Growing in Humility

The words of the Prophet Micah summarize what the Lord requires of us: "to do justice, and to love kindness, and to walk humbly with [our] God" (Mi 6:8).

Humility motivates us to prefer the path that leads us to eternal life. It keeps us from closing ourselves off from pursuing the task the Spirit inspires us to fulfill here and now. The vices of pride and disobedience, on the other hand, block openness to this truth. These vices come with our fallen condition. They alienate us from God's will and from one another. We pretend to appreciate people, events, and things, but we only do so to use them to make us look better, despite the pernicious outcomes that result from a life of lying.

Openness does not allow us to exclude any facet of the truth. The only way to overcome bad choices is to face them and then try to grow beyond them. Closed-off, proud, humorless people decide in advance what they shall and shall not allow to touch them. They are loath to listen to constructive criticism and the grain of truth it usually contains. They would rather organize their lives around measurable, utilitarian projects than risk losing control. Such rigidity may close them off from any message not directly relevant to their functionalistic demands for success at any price.

When our attention to smooth functioning excludes other facets of formation, it becomes difficult, if not impossible, to grow through the graces of openness, humility, and humor. Such a one-sided existence gives rise to isolation and fragmentation, to chronic murmuring and complaining. These negative dispositions harm the formation of our faith community as a whole, as well as each member of it.

Growing in Humor

Humility comes from the same Latin root as *humus*, meaning "earth" or "ground." It seems to suggest that we should be open to our earthiness, that is to say, to the reality of our always fallible personhood. Humor helps us to overcome the tendency to blow things out of proportion under the pressure of the lust for power.

Wise friends and servants of the Lord use timely humor to deflate any exaltation that may creep into their ministry. Amusing anecdotes break into a seriousness that could puff us up with our own importance. Spontaneous laughter reminds us of the amusing precariousness of life. A comic remark or an unexpected, playful response to a question frees us from the threat of taking ourselves too seriously.

Walking the narrow way allows us to engage lightheartedly in our life story. We find that the key to enjoying our journey is a humorous give-and-take between us and our companions in Christ. The twinkle of an eye and the flash of a smile are sure to counteract arrogance and put intellectual smugness in its place. God help us if cool logic and willful determination dominate our days by stifling spontaneity and relaxed openness! Hearty laughter relaxes our fixation on having to pursue instant saint-hood.

Humor is good medicine; it reminds us that stress lessens when we try to be playful. As a result, we usually get more work done. Seeing the comical side of an uptight situation may diffuse its intensity and clear the way for more creative solutions.

Humor lets us admit our vulnerability rather than trying to hide our imperfections. Sharing the same sad-funny moments makes us feel more accepted. We do not laugh at one another but with one another. Through the gift of laughter, we learn to relativize our troubles and help others do the same.

We need the balm of their kindness to offset the meanness that at times surrounds us. Since the Lord is kind and faithful to us (see 2 Sm 2:6), why can't we show the same courtesy to others? Do we really need to engage in obnoxious behavior? Is it necessary to pin pejorative labels on other people? Is it not part of our calling in Christ to offset the unkindness shown by tyrants who rant and rave when anyone dares to oppose their condemnatory tactics?

Meanness cancels mercy, just as cynicism destroys humility and humor. Thank God the Lord is kind to us when so many others may not be! Perhaps they do not realize how deeply their snide remarks hurt us. Even acts of kindness on our part may only arouse their suspicion.

How refreshing, by contrast, God's faithfulness is! It makes us smile to remember that every time we stray, God calls us to come home. No matter how many times we break our promises, God invites us to try again to keep them. God does not give up on us. Rather, the Lord leaves the ninety-nine sheep behind to search and to find the lamb he has lost. And so we pray:

Lord, help us to live

in gratefulness for your gifts
outpoured on teeming shores
of generosity beyond imagining.

Make us adore
the mystery of Holy Energy,
of God-given potency
playing in cosmos and humanity.

Let us
bend our knee
before the daily gift
of Eucharist:
your body and blood,
soul and divinity
granted to all who believe
every time we receive.

Pause and Ponder

- If I were asked to list the joys of walking the narrow way, what would be the first three items on my list?
- What episodes of late have most helped me to learn that without humility no progress in the life of the spirit is possible?

STEP TWELVE
Rejoicing in a Life of Fidelity to the Lord

Moving Toward Union with the Trinity

I am your servant; give me understanding,
so that I may know your decrees.

Psalm 119:125

In his letter to the Ephesians, Saint Paul prays that the end for which we have journeyed on the narrow way will lead us to the full glory of union with the Trinity: "I pray that you may have the power to comprehend, with all the saints, what is the breadth and length and height and depth, and to know the love of Christ that surpasses knowledge, so that you may be filled with all the fullness of God" (Eph 3:18–19).

What else is this "fullness" than the consummation of love that is meant to be ours as adopted children of God? All formation from birth to death finds its ultimate origin in the Father through whom all that is has come to be. This transition from our essence in the Father to our existence in time is the crowning achievement of the Incarnate Word, the Second Person of the Blessed Trinity. The Divine Son resides in our hearts. In faith we hear and heed his call. With the inspired knowledge granted to us through his Bride, the Church, we come to the realization that our origination in the Father and our redemption from slavery to sin through the Son becomes possible thanks to our Sanctifier, the Holy Spirit.

In this way, the fullness of God finds its home in the spirit, heart, mind, and will of every baptized soul. As these graces mature in us, the Spirit moves us to go into the world and proclaim the Good News of Christ's transforming power with a joy that no one can take from us (see Jn 16:22).

This transformation so moves us that we dare to pray:

> You came to us, Lord Jesus, not to return alone into the silent splendor of the Trinity but to take us with you. You came among us to share with us your life of love and to so change us that, sinners though we are, we might be able to know in faith our Father as you know him, because you and the Father are one (Jn 10:22–30). You came into this world to lead us through the narrow gate, and now, at journey's end, you bring us home to eternal life, to intimacy with the mystery of the Trinity.

From this wellspring of prayer arises the awareness that despite our frailty and fears, God is in us and we are in God. Whatever obstacles life may place on our path, however lost and confused we may be, this pledge of union and communion never changes. God will not leave us orphaned (see Jn 14:18). Through stillness and listening, through reflection and prayer, we embody Christ's gift of peace in our personal and communal lives.

For us to enter into these depths of divine love, what has to die is not our deepest self, but the false self that originates when we pretend to be all-powerful. That is why on the twelfth rung of the ladder, Saint Benedict returns to his essential teaching that we should try always to manifest humility in our decisions and deeds, since this virtue is our greatest safeguard against the illusion of self-sufficiency.

To move toward union with the Trinity, we need to shed the imprisoning restrictions of self-centeredness and acknowledge anew our dependence on God; we may then be able to relinquish over a lifetime the obstacles that stand between us and whatever we have made ultimate besides our Lord. As long as we cling to anything or anyone less than God, we can never experience the liberation of soaring without hindrance to our Beloved.

Living in Fidelity to the Lord

Our desire to live in fidelity to the Lord prompts us to foster the style of life depicted by the apostle Paul: "Put on then, as God's chosen ones, holy and beloved, heartfelt compassion, kindness, humility, gentleness, and patience, bearing with one another and forgiving one another. … And over all these put on love, that is, the bond of perfection" (Col 3:12–14, NABRE).

The best of two worlds opens before us at this juncture of our journey on the narrow way: We pay attention to God's guidance in stillness, and we spend our energy doing good works. God escorts us through a maze of daily demands, showing us how to maintain the peace of Christ, even when life moves at a hectic pace.

If contemplation is the reservoir of our soul, then charity is the canal that flows from it. Only when we root our service of others in contemplative presence can we avoid working as a means to attain successful outcomes with little or no consideration of making the sacrifices God may ask of us.

Contemplation enables us to be present *in* the world without succumbing to the ways *of* the world. We plant our feet on the firm ground of God's love while going forth in labors for the kingdom. First in this line of discipline is *faith*. To live by it is to confirm the veracity of God's promise that he will fill an empty jar with oil (see 2 Kgs 4:1–7); that a virgin will give birth to a son; and that he will restore sight to the blind (see Tb 11:7–8).

Guided by the Trinity

Though we may not expect it, we may sense that the Triune God bestows upon us an embrace of love that can be momentarily overwhelming. St. John of the Cross (1542–1591) touches upon this mystery in his masterpiece, *The Living Flame of Love.* He says that this flame, like the tongues of fire at Pentecost, is the Holy Spirit. Its effect is paradoxical: it burns, but it is also benevolent. Every time it flares up, it consumes lingering traces of selfish sensuality and strengthens our commitment to live contemplatively and to act charitably.

If the soil of peace is a broken, humbled heart, then its harvest is a disciplined, ordered sense of receptivity to God's will and a willingness to advance Christ's reign in this world. Resting in God grants our once restless heart the experience of coming home to the Holy.

The fruits of contemplative stillness reveal a preference for silence rather than the babble of empty words. We seek solitude instead of losing ourselves in a faceless crowd or a leveling collectivity. Out of this peace comes the thoughtfulness to explore whether or not we *ought* to do something, even if, technically speaking, we *can* do it.

Contemplatives keep alive the sense of mystery that surrounds the delicate yet demanding experience of union with the Trinity. They are unafraid to counter any form of dehumanization or depletion of human and natural resources. They are in a sense "ecologists of the spirit," who preserve the truths and teachings they find in Scripture and the masters.

Is there any lasting response to the question of what direction God intends our life to take? What influences our life more or less continuously, albeit often in hidden ways, is the mystery of our deepest calling in, with, and through Christ. It is at the root of the various transitory positions and relationships within which we have to express who we are and what we hope to become.

The more our spiritual life progresses, the more we are able to behold existence as a pattern of providential events. It is not a haphazard collection of accidental happenings. When we view the course of our journey so far, we see that what the Trinitarian mystery is weaving always takes into account our successive life situations. What remains a lasting fruit is the invitation to personal holiness that comes to us from the Lord. This deepest *within* refers to our inmost nobility to be and become another Christ. This at-homeness with who we are most deeply is never selfish or exclusive; it pours itself out in inclusive care and compassion for others.

Such intimacy goes beyond cordial interactions with others that are here today and gone tomorrow. Instead, our being with and for one another enriches our times of togetherness. We feel so in tune that we are able to converse about whatever providential circumstances we incur along the narrow way. Amid a range of mutual setbacks and successes, we experience a growing conviction of God's presence in and around us.

Extending the Blessings of Union with the Trinity to Others

Saint Elizabeth of the Trinity (1880–1906), as her name reveals, enjoyed the lasting fruits of intimacy with the Father, Son, and Holy Spirit from whom she received inspired gifts.

Her expression of this mysterious indwelling of the Trinity in our soul is her most vivid personal memory and the key to her spiritual doctrine.

From an early age until she became a Carmelite nun, Saint Elizabeth professed to have found heaven on earth. Young as she was when she died from Addison's disease, she left a remarkable body of writings woven around the central theme that because God is in our soul, we can live as if we were already in eternity.

"Sabeth" loved the epistles of Paul and found in them confirmation of her deepest desire for union with God. For instance, he says in Philippians 3:20, "our citizenship is in heaven, and it is from there that we are expecting a Savior, the Lord Jesus Christ." He then goes on to say: "He will transform the body of our humiliation that it may be conformed to the body of his glory, by the power that also enables him to make all things subject to himself. Therefore, my brothers and sisters, whom I love and long for, my joy and crown, stand firm in the Lord in this way" (Phil 3:21—4:1).

For Saint Elizabeth, the narrow way meant to wait upon the Lord with a servant's heart. Only then can we discern his voice among the many voices pulling us from the right path. Her prayer was to become God's partner and to encourage all disciples to be faithful to the heavenly calling that was theirs (see Heb 3:1). Obscure as her vocation as a Carmelite nun was in the eyes of the world, Elizabeth gave the Lord so much room to work in her soul that there was no way to stop his creative action in her life.

In her prayer to the Holy Trinity, which she composed in 1903, she lifts up the lasting fruits of pursuing intimacy with Three Persons in one God, beginning with *self-forgetfulness*. She prays, "Help me to forget myself entirely that I may be established in You." A second fruit is that her soul may be as still and peaceful as if she were already in eternity. She asks God for a great favor: "May nothing trouble my peace or make me leave You, O my unchanging One, but may each minute carry me further into the depths of Your Mystery." Elizabeth then begs for the grace of being vigilant, adoring, and docile to God's every movement in her spirit, heart, mind, and will. She is under no illusion. She is as weak a soul as God can find, which is why she needs clothing with the strength of Christ, her Savior. She asks for the grace to listen to him, to remain "wholly teachable" that he may show her everything she needs to know to never withdraw from his radiance. Elizabeth's prayer concludes with these unforgettable words:

O Consuming Fire, Spirit of Love, "come upon me,"
and create in my soul a kind of incarnation of the Word:
that I may be another humanity for Him in whom He can
renew His whole Mystery. ... O my Three, my all, my
Beatitude, infinite Solitude, Immensity in which I lose
myself, I surrender myself to You as Your prey. Bury
Yourself in me that I may bury myself in You until I
depart to contemplate in Your light the abyss of Your
greatness. Amen.

Our communion with the Trinity proves that God has a special purpose for our life and that it will reveal itself with the passage of time. Whether we break bread at the dinner table or celebrate the Eucharist together, we witness to the coming transformation of the world by the fruit of Trinitarian intimacy. Blessings abound when we put aside bothersome attachments and face life's challenges with equanimity.

As we detach ourselves from the self we used to be, it may feel as if we have died a little. This is a normal experience on the narrow way. It is the same feeling that grips us when we leave a place we love, never to return, or when we have to endure the permanent parting caused by a beloved person's death. Such detachment, powerful as it is, is not avoidable. In a sense, we die a little every day we are alive.

There is no use in our searching for the perfect home on earth when what awaits us is that joyous homecoming that is beyond the present life. We must be careful not to attach too much significance to any feeling of nesting in safety, for all such experiences pass away. Only one homecoming leads us to the Father's house, and that is the heavenly shelter we Christians must ultimately seek.

Buoyed up by the power of this revelation, we pass from paying too much attention to externals to meditating on the meanings they conceal. Such attention marks the moment of conversion from a cursory life to a contemplative vision of living in union with the Trinity. This loving mutuality fills us with adoration. What a blessing it is to share the gratefulness that floods our being as we pray:

Mighty currents of formation
    emanate from you,
    O Trinity:
A mystical tide
sweeps invisibly
through space and time,
humanity and history,
inundating all becoming,
giving rise to countless forms
    of life and matter,
synchronized in the Father's
enfleshed eternal Word
in whom we dwell,
    who dwells in us

lifting us lovingly
into your mystery,
O Trinity.

Pause and Ponder

- When I walk the narrow way, do I feel like a companion of the Trinity? Do I pray for guidance to the Father, the Son, and the Holy Spirit?
- Have I begun to taste and savor more intimacy with the Trinity? In what way has this encounter with the mystery of transforming love changed my life?

CONCLUSION
The Christian Life as a Prelude to a Good Death

Holy Mary, Mother of God, pray for us
sinners now and at the hour of our death.
Amen.

Every time we pray the "Hail Mary," along with our other deeply loved prayers and devotions, we ask for the grace of a good death. Our passing may or may not be without physical debilitation. Ours might be a sudden end in an accident or a natural disaster. However the end comes, there is no escape. That is why we beg for the grace to say until our last breath, "Where, O death, is your victory? / Where, O death, is your sting?" (1 Cor 15:55, NABRE).

Despite the depth of our faith, fear of death is part of life. Being afraid to die is a normal response to the unknown. Faith in God, especially when we have eschewed the comforts of the wide path and chosen the hard road, enables us to advance toward death and dying in prayerful surrender.

We submit our fears to the power of redeeming love. We believe that God shall lift us into the light of longed-for union with him. We see our death, thanks to Christ's victory, not as an end but as a new beginning. Faith in his resurrection from the dead gives us the courage to look upon our own death as but a brief passage from life to Life.

The two years prior to the death of Fr. Adrian van Kaam on November 17, 2007, remain in my memory forever. By the summer of 2005, his mobility had deteriorated to such a degree that it was necessary to transfer him to the assisted living center of the Holy Ghost Fathers, where he resided until his already fading health, caused mainly by a chronic heart condition, further eroded due to a severe fall that resulted in a bad break of his left arm. On the advice of his medical doctors, he moved to the skilled care facility of the Little Sisters of the Poor in Pittsburgh. There he lived in the Sacred Heart Residence for two more years in serene acceptance of his "crucifying epiphany."

During this time, he did what he could to encourage everyone who visited him (I did so almost daily on behalf of the Epiphany Association we cofounded in 1979) to stand firm on the foundations of our faith; to maintain the highest level of integrity in our personal lives and in our service to others; and to adhere to the truth that makes us free (see Jn 8:32). These are the lights by which Father Adrian lived; they are the legacy he left us when he breathed his last and entered his heavenly home.

Remarkably, despite failing health and relapses in vocal and mental acuity, he was able to dictate to me several poems pertaining to his "crucifying epiphany." One of the most remarkable is "Joy in the Dying," which expresses his hope for a good death. He writes:

> Lord, let me behold
>   the last beautiful
>   moment of my life
>   in this world.

Earthly life shows
　　its face to me
　　and I rejoice
　　benevolently.
Your preparation
　　of my poor heart
　　and soul for this moment
　　evokes thanks
　　in my whole being
　　whose hard edges
　　you have refined.

Thank you, Lord of life,
　　for granting me
　　amidst this strife
　　a final consolation,
　　quelling the last
　　traces of my anxiety,
　　letting none of it
　　be left in me.

The first part of Father Adrian's poem teaches us that the anxiety we feel can be the Lord's way of calling us to face our finitude and to deepen our faith in God. Looked at from a merely human perspective, death means a separation from all we hold most dear. As Father lay dying, I held one of his hands and the president of our board of directors held the other, while the sisters gathered around his bed and sang like an angelic choir the *Salve Regina*.

Father left behind not only the rigors of aging and severe illness but also this inspiring message, captured in the second part of his poem:

Overwhelming every fiber

of my being is a feeling
of pure joy.
In gratefulness you allow me
to grow still, to contemplate
life's beauty, to move
into the depths of this good-bye
to my beloved earth,
to enter the kairos time
of eternal ecstasy.

Thank you, my Beloved,
for this — the greatest
of all gifts — to relinquish
fear and ready myself
to receive you fully.

Now — by your grace —
I forget about anxiety
and insecurity. I ready
my poverty for the
irresistible joy of eternity.
Let us go hand and hand
into the clouds
of endless beauty,
to that place
of unspeakable grace
where you await me
for all of eternity.

Such dispositions, bolstered by faith and trust in God, recon-
firmed what it means to choose the hard road that leads in the
end to the consolations of discipleship. It is the Lord who shep-
herds us through life and teaches us the art and discipline of

relinquishing any semblance of our being in ultimate control.

As Father Adrian obeyed the Father's will, so must we, until the moment he calls us to pass over from the temporal to the eternal. Being with a beloved person in this final hour, as we were with Father Adrian, elicits a deeper, indeed an indelible, awareness of our dependence on God; it announces once again a call to conversion and radical recommitment to the Father, the Son, and the Holy Spirit in whose name we make the Sign of the Cross — a powerful moment of anointing at the closure of our earthly window.

Father Adrian taught us that life is a gift to enjoy until the time comes for us to surrender it into a mightier Hand. Thus he sings in his poem:

> Like an excited child
> I dare to sing
> this hymn of welcome
> to Sister Death.
> How often we shall
> repeat this song
> when we are together
> in heaven.

Daily we live through little deaths — disappointments, misunderstandings, and painful but hopefully passing illnesses. They make us aware of the fact that we are vulnerable and finite children of God. We need both the active strength to rise to these challenges and the passive strength to endure them until they pass. Every time we cultivate holy fear, the first step on the way to entering the narrow gate, we live in awe of the mystery of the dying and rising of Jesus that points to the ultimate meaning of our life. Christ's peace and joy invade our soul, and we pray with Father Adrian:

Joy, joy, joy.
My spirit waits upon
your loving presence,
as we dance with enthusiasm
in a tender embrace.
I sing a song of welcome
to your invitation. You
have made my child-like
soul full of sweet elation,
and I thank you for this meditation.

Being somber about my end
is not necessary.
I long to see your face
amidst choirs
of singing angels
in the presence
of everyone I have ever loved.
With palms waving in their hands,
they will welcome me,
and together we will absorb
the goodness of the Lord.
Shed from us like dead skin
will be the "what ifs" of
shadowy doubts that signify
the last remnants
of the devil in us.
We shall radiate
our true form, the wholeness
of spirit that is the best
that can happen to us
poor pilgrims on the way

to our true home.

How lovely holy dying really is.

Such a view of what it means to listen to Jesus and follow his call gives us the courage to face the truth that no one can die our death for us. We must make this leap of faith on our own into the unknown heavenly home from whence there is no return. Having followed in the footsteps of Jesus, we believe, as Father Adrian did, that Christ has prepared a place for us in his Father's house (see Jn 14:1–3). To focus our attention on this promise allays our natural fears of death and dying and assures us that we will fall at the last intake of breath into the waiting arms of our Lord, praying as we depart:

How I long to hear you
whisper words of gentle
consolation: My child,
take heart. I am so
happy with your soul.
Your time has come
in accordance with my will.
Enter the gates my Father
has opened to you. Come in
and be freed
from the ravages of sin,
come in to the place
in Father's house
I have reserved for you
from the beginning,
before you came to be.
Amen.

My prayer is that the road map depicted in this book and inspired by Chapter Seven of the *Rule of Saint Benedict* has helped us to awaken to the reality that from the moment of conception to the moment of death, the Trinity has adopted us into a relationship of exquisite intimacy with the Father, Son, and Holy Spirit.

The conditions for this awakening are: obeying the word of the Lord; abiding by the directives of discipleship; and remaining open to the grace of transformation in Christ.

To evade the wide path and choose the hard road, the four counsels we must follow are: to confess our faults and weaknesses; to practice the peace of Jesus; to put on the mind of Christ; and to offer care in his name.

When we enter through the narrow gate, our life changes for the better insofar as we listen more than we speak; revitalize our faith community; celebrate the gift of appreciative living; and move toward union with the Trinity.

For these and many other reasons this book has meditated upon, may we come to understand why living with Christ is and always will be a victory over death and a portal to heaven.

> Do not let your hearts be troubled. Believe in God, believe also in me. In my Father's house there are many dwelling places. If it were not so, would I have told you that I go to prepare a place for you? And if I go and prepare a place for you, I will come again and will take you to myself, so that where I am, there you may be also. (John 14:1–3)

Bibliography of Recommended Readings

Augustine of Hippo. St. *The Confessions of St. Augustine*. Translated by John K. Ryan. Garden City, NY: Image Books, 1960.

Benedict, Saint. *Rule of St. Benedict: Insights for the Ages*. Edited by Joan D. Chittister. New York: Crossroad, 1993.

Bonhoeffer, Dietrich. *The Cost of Discipleship*. New York, NY: Touchstone, 1995.

Ciszek, Walter J., SJ, with Daniel Flaherty. *He Leadeth Me*. Garden City, NY: Image Books, Doubleday, 1975.

Creasy, William C. *The Imitation of Christ by Thomas à Kempis*. Notre Dame, IN: Ave Maria Press, 1989.

Elizabeth of the Trinity. St. *Elizabeth of the Trinity: The Complete Works*. Vol. 1, *General Introduction and Major Spiritual Writings*. Translated by Aletheia Kane. Washington, DC: ICS Publications, 1984.

———. St. *Elizabeth of the Trinity: The Complete Works*. Vol. 2, *Letters from Carmel*. Translated by Anne Englund Nash. Washington, DC: ICS Publications, 1995.

Frossard, André. *"Forget Not Love": The Passion of Maximilian Kolbe*. Translated by Cendrine Fontan. San Francisco, CA: Ignatius Press, 1991.

John of the Cross. St. *The Living Flame of Love* in *The Collected Works of St. John of the Cross.* Translated by Kieran Kavanaugh and Otilio Rodriguez. Washington, DC: ICS Publications, 1991.

Kowalska, Maria Faustina. St. *Divine Mercy in My Soul.* Stockbridge, MA: Marian Press–Association of Marian Helpers, 1981.

Br. Lawrence of the Resurrection. *The Practice of the Presence of God.* Critical Edition, Conrad De Meester. Translated by Salvatore Sciurba. Washington, DC: ICS Publications, 1994.

Muto, Susan. *A Heart for Hungry Soul: Lessons from the Church's Greatest Masters and Mystics.* Notre Dame, IN: Ave Maria Press, 2020.

———. *Meditation in Motion: Finding the Mystery in Ordinary Moments.* Pittsburgh, PA: Epiphany Books, 2001.

———. *Blessings that Make Us Be: A Formative Approach to Living the Beatitudes.* Pittsburgh, PA: Epiphany Books, 2002.

———. *Dear Master: Letters on Spiritual Direction Inspired by St. John of the Cross. A Companion to The Living Flame of Love.* Pittsburgh, PA: Epiphany Books, 2004.

———. *Drop Your Nets and Follow Jesus: How to Form Disciples for the New Evangelization.* Hyde Park, NY: New City Press, 2019.

———. *Gratefulness: The Habit of a Grace-Filled Life.* Notre Dame, IN: Ave Maria Press, 2018.

———. *The Life Journey of a Joyful Man of God: The Autobiographical Memoirs of Adrian van Kaam.* Eugene, OR: Resource Publications, 2011.

———. *Virtues: Your Christian Legacy.* Steubenville, OH: Emmaus Road, 2014.

Ten Boom, Corrie. *The Hiding Place.* Grand Rapids, MI: Chosen Books, 1971.

Teresa of Ávila. *The Way of Perfection.* In *The Collected Works of St. Teresa of Avila.* Vol. 2. Translated by Kieran Kavanaugh and Otilio Rodriguez. Washington, DC: ICS Publications, 1980.

Thérèse of Lisieux. *Story of A Soul: The Autobiography of St. Thérèse of Lisieux.* Translated by John Clarke. Washington, DC: ICS Publications, 1975.

van Kaam, Adrian, and Susan Muto. *Readings from A to Z: The Poetry of Epiphany.* Pittsburgh, PA: Epiphany, 2000.

———. *Divine Guidance: Seeking to Find and Follow the Will of God.* Pittsburgh, PA: Epiphany Books, 2000.

———. *Christian Articulation of the Mystery. Formation Theology,* Vol. 2. Pittsburgh, PA: Epiphany Association, 2005.

———. *Formation of the Christian Heart. Formation Theology,* Vol. 3. Pittsburgh, PA: Epiphany Association, 2006.

———. *Foundations of Christian Formation. Formation Theology,* Vol. 1. Pittsburgh, PA: Epiphany Association, 2004.

———. *Living Our Christian Faith and Formation Traditions. Formation Theology,* Vol. 4. Pittsburgh, PA: Epiphany Association, 2007.

———. *Practicing the Prayer of Presence.* Williston Park, NY: Resurrection Press, 1993.

———. *The Commandments: Ten Ways to a Happy Life and a Healthy Soul.* Ann Arbor, MI: Servant Publications, 1996.

About the Author

Susan Muto, Ph.D., is executive director of the Epiphany Association, based in Pittsburgh, Pennsylvania, and dean of the Epiphany Academy of Formative Spirituality. She holds a doctorate in English literature from the University of Pittsburgh, where she specialized in the work of post-Reformation spiritual writers. From 1966 to 1988, she served in various administrative and teaching positions at the Institute of Formative Spirituality (IFS) at Duquesne University and lectured nationally and internationally then and now on the classical masters of the Judeo-Christian faith and formation traditions.

Dr. Muto has been teaching the literature of ancient, medieval, and modern spirituality for over forty years. She has also recorded popular audio and video series. All of these resources are available in the bookstore section of www.epiphanyassociation.org.

Her articles have appeared in *Catholic Library World, Mount Carmel, The Priest* magazine, and *Human Development*. She has written more than thirty books of her own and many others co-authored with Fr. Adrian van Kaam, CSSp, Ph.D. (1920–2007). Her companion texts to the masterpieces of St. John of the Cross complement her latest book, *A Feast for Hungry Souls: Spiritual Lessons from the Church's Greatest Masters and Mystics* (Notre

Dame, IN: Ave Maria Press, 2020), winner of the 2021 first place award in spirituality from the Catholic Media Association.

In addition to many rewards and an honorary degree from King's College, she received in 2014 the Aggiornamento Award presented by the Catholic Library Association in recognition of an outstanding contribution made by an individual or an organization to the ministry of renewal modeled by Pope St. John XXIII.

About the Poet

Fr. Adrian van Kaam, CSSp, Ph.D. (1920-2007), is the originator of formation science and its underlying formation anthropology, new disciplines that serve his systematic formation theology. Taken as a whole, all three fields comprise the art and discipline of formative spirituality.

He inaugurated this unique approach in Holland in the 1940s. Upon coming to the United States in 1954, he went to Case Western Reserve University in Cleveland, where he received his doctorate in psychology. Shortly thereafter, he became an American citizen. From 1954 to 1963, he taught his original approach to psychology as a human science at Duquesne University. In 1963 he founded the graduate Institute of Formative Spirituality, received the President's Award for excellence in research, and taught there as a professor in the field until its closing in 1993. He was also the recipient of an honorary Doctor of Christian Letters degree from the Franciscan University of Steubenville, Ohio.

In 1979 he cofounded with Dr. Susan Muto the Epiphany Association and its worldwide mission and ministry. Father Adrian was a renowned speaker, an inspiration to many, the author of more than sixty books on spiritual formation, and a prolific poet whose works enjoy worldwide recognition.

Other Books by the Author

A Feast for Hungry Souls: Spiritual Lessons from the Church's Greatest Masters and Mystics

Approaching the Sacred: An Introduction to Spiritual Reading

A Practical Guide to Spiritual Reading

Blessings that Make Us Be: A Formative Approach to Living the Beatitudes

Caring for the Caregiver

Catholic Spirituality A to Z: An Inspirational Dictionary

Celebrating the Single Life: A Spirituality for Single Persons in Today's World

Dear Master: Letters on Spiritual Direction Inspired by St. John of the Cross

Deep into the Thicket: Soul-Searching Meditations Inspired by St. John of the Cross

Drop Your Nets and Follow Jesus: How to Form Disciples for the New Evangelization

Gratefulness: The Habit of a Grace-Filled Life

John of the Cross for Today: The Ascent

John of the Cross for Today: The Dark Night

Keepsakes for the Journey: Four Weeks on Faith Deepening

Late Have I Loved Thee: The Recovery of Intimacy
Meditation in Motion: Finding the Mystery in Ordinary Moments
One in the Lord: Living Our Call to Christian Community
Pathways of Spiritual Living
Praying the Lord's Prayer with Mary
Renewed at Each Awakening
Steps Along the Way: The Path of Spiritual Reading
Table of Plenty: Good Food for Body and Soul
The Journey Homeward
Then God Said: Contemplating the First Revelation in Creation
Twelve Little Ways to Transform Your Heart: Lessons in Holiness and Evangelization from St. Thérèse of Lisieux
Virtues: Your Christian Legacy
Where Lovers Meet: Inside the Interior Castle
Where Your Treasure Is: The Last Spiritual Counsels of a Modern Master, Father Adrian van Kaam
Womanspirit: Reclaiming the Deep Feminine in Our Human Spirituality
Words of Wisdom for Our World: The Precautions and Counsels of St. John of the Cross